ORIGINS

OF THE

BLACK PRESS

New York, 1827-1847

ORIGINS

—— OF THE ——

BLACK PRESS

New York, 1827-1847

by Bernell Tripp

VISION PRESS

Published by
Vision Press
P.O. Box 1106
3230 Mystic Lake Way
Northport, Alabama 35476

Library of Congress Cataloguing-in-Publication Data

Tripp, Bernell, 1960-
    Origins of the Black press : New York, 1827-1847 /
    Bernell Tripp.
        p.   cm.
    Includes index.
    ISBN 0-9630700-1-0 : $10.00
    1. Afro-American press--New York (State)--History--
    19th century.
    I. Title.
    PN4882.5.T75   1992
    071'.3'08996--dc20   91-44005
                                                                      CIP

Printed in the United States of America

CONTENTS

ORIGINS

—— OF THE ——

BLACK PRESS

New York, 1827-1847

Introduction

ORIGINS OF THE BLACK PRESS

When the first issue of *Freedom's Journal* reached the citizens of New York on March 16, 1827, black journalism was almost seven generations behind its white counterpart, which already had been in existence for 137 years. The majority of the potential black audience lived in the South as slaves, isolated and illiterate. In some Southern states it was still illegal to teach a black person to read, and interference with the distribution of reading material to blacks was the norm in many other areas.

In the North, the atmosphere was slightly different, particularly in New York City. New York had a sizeable population of free blacks and former slaves, both escaped and freed. While the abolitionist movement was not as strong as in Boston or Philadelphia, many whites did not openly oppose blacks and the antislavery issue, despite vituperate attacks against the blacks by several New York newspapers.

Over the years, historians have supported the idea that this opposition to slavery served as the primary reason for the establishment of approximately 40 black newspapers founded by black Americans in the United States prior to the Civil War. In other words, these weeklies were considered to be a means of expressing black Americans' distaste and opposition to the enslavement of their brothers and sisters.

However, slavery was only one of many issues confronting a race fragmented by varying levels of education, as well as economic and social standing. Other factors besides slavery—such as improving the lifestyle of blacks or developing a type of racial cohesiveness—might have motivated many early black journalists. Some of these factors may have been of a higher priority to black editors and publishers such as Samuel Cornish, John Russwurm, and Martin Delany. Such priorities would indeed have had an impact on the newspapers' content.

The stated purposes of these newspapers placed a greater emphasis on civil rights, pride, unity and the progress of the black race. Since it was highly improbable that the papers could ever reach the slaves or any population in the South, the messages were directed toward those free blacks in the North—the group with the more pressing need for guidance.

Editors and publishers of the early black press were already community and church leaders, and the newspapers they created reflected this sense of obligation. *Freedom's Journal, Weekly Advocate, Ram's Horn*, and the *North Star* were founded in New York over a 20-year period between 1827 and 1847, existing long enough to exert considerable influence over the black community and other members of the black press. *Freedom's Journal* and the *Weekly Advocate* were both under the direction of Samuel Cornish. The *Ram's Horn*, though created by Willis Hodges, was noted for one of its more prominent contributors, Frederick Douglass. Douglass later founded the *North Star*.

It is also significant that all four papers originated in New York rather than Boston or Philadelphia, towns in which large black populations resided. In the latter two cities, sympathy toward blacks was extremely high, particularly in Philadelphia, where there existed one of the strongest white abolitionist groups. However, in New York several white newspapers exhibited strong objections to abolition and to certain aspects of the black community. Therefore, black newspapers there were some of the first to challenge a society in which lines of opposition were clearly established.

1

FREEDOM'S JOURNAL: THE BEGINNING

By the 1820s, the black population in the North was made up of free blacks and runaway slaves, all seeking a better way of life. Many had received a formal education, while others possessed only rudimentary abilities in reading and writing. However, all blacks seemed eager to accept a black newspaper devoted to their particular needs, since few white editors were willing to allow them access to mainstream newspaper columns.

Into this climate the Rev. Samuel Cornish and John Russwurm, two black free men, introduced *Freedom's Journal*. Historians have speculated that the inception of *Freedom's Journal* was "the result of a meeting of Messrs. Russwurm, Cornish and others at the house of M. Bostin Crummell...in New York, called to consider the attacks of...a local paper published in New York City...by an Afro-American-hating Jew, which made the vilest attacks on the Afro-Americans."[1]

---

[1]Irving Garland Penn, *The Afro-American Press and Its Editors* (Springfield, Mass.: Wiley and Co., 1891), 27-28.

The "Afro-American-hating Jew" was Mordecai M. Noah of the New York *Enquirer*. After reading Noah's attacks, Cornish and Russwurm responded with letters to the editor of the *Enquirer* and were denied publication. Outraged at being denied a voice, the two pooled their resources and began publishing *Freedom's Journal.*[2]

Neither of the two men possessed any newspaper experience. Cornish was a Presbyterian minister born in Delaware and reared in Philadelphia and New York. He organized the first black Presbyterian Church on New Demeter Street in Manhattan after his graduation from the Free African School.[3] Russwurm, a half-black Jamaican, was a graduate of Bowdoin College, one of the first blacks to graduate from any college in the United States. Previously, Russwurm had planned to study medicine in Boston before emigrating to Haiti.[4] However, following graduation he moved to New York, where he met Cornish and other black leaders of the period and agreed to the proposal of establishing a newspaper.

The *Journal* itself usually consisted of four pages numbered consecutively from issue to issue, which included four columns on 10-by-15 inch paper. The paper appeared weekly on Fridays and was priced at $3 per year, payable half

---

[2]See Bella Gross, "'Freedom's Journal' and the 'Rights of All,'" *Journal of Negro History* 17 (July 1932): 243; Lauren Kessler, *The Dissident Press: Alternative Journalism in American History* (Beverly Hills: Sage Publications, 1984), 28.

[3]Lerone Bennett, Jr., *Pioneers in Protest* (Chicago: Johnson Publishing Co., 1968), 60.

[4]John B. Russwurm to Col. John S. Russwurm, 9 January 1826, Original in Ms Section, Tennessee State Library and Archives; copy in Bowdoin College Library.

yearly in advance, or $2.50 if paid in full.

The paper contained some original articles, as well as items "lifted" from other newspapers—a commonly accepted practice during the period. Usually only about two of the sixteen columns of reading material in each issue were devoted to current news. The remaining columns contained such items as personal profiles, moral lessons, poetry, and advertisements. Numerous black leaders contributed sermons, speeches, and articles on scientific, educational, and political topics. Biblical excerpts and religious parables provided inspiration. Domestic and foreign news items reported meetings of black citizens, crimes against slaves, slavery in other countries, ship sailings, and other miscellaneous occurrences.

Even though slavery was among the topics addressed in the columns of *Freedom's Journal*, it was not a primary concern. In an environment which was reluctant to support black progress, it is unlikely that the paper could afford to be too outspoken against slavery. Considering that the paper would probably never reach the slaves or free blacks of the South, Cornish and Russwurm concerned themselves primarily with the blacks in the North and the development of racial unity and progress.

The first issue of *Freedom's Journal*, complete with its slogan "Righteousness Exalteth a Nation," was not exactly a major force in the abolitionist movement—a movement which had not taken hold by 1827. Two articles were indicative of the intent of the publication—one depicted the "Memoirs of Capt. Paul Cuffee," a successful black fisherman; and the other was a reprint of "People of Colour" (clipped from the *Christian Spectator*) which examined slavery as a legal institution. The first emphasized the progress of blacks, while the latter was more of an *appeal* to examine the issue of slavery, rather than a *demand* for action.

Slavery was only one of the subjects addressed by the editors of the *Journal*. Cornish and Russwurm also concerned themselves with providing a forum for black protest, as well as promoting such things as striving to achieve financial success and strong moral character in order to gain acceptance by a white society.[5]

A good example of the *Journal* editors' commitment to fulfilling a variety of objectives was revealed in the paper's first editorial, "To Our Patrons," which served as a statement of purpose. The editorial read in part:

> We wish to plead our cause. Too long have others spoken for us. Too long has the publick been deceived by misrepresentations, in things which concern us dearly, though in the estimation of some mere trifles; for though there are many in society who exercise towards us benevolent feelings; still (with sorrow we confess it) there are others who make it their business to enlarge upon the least trifle, which tends to the discredit of any person of colour; and pronounce anathemas and denounce our whole body for the misconduct of this guilty one. We are aware that there are many instances of vice among us, but we avow that it is because no one has taught its subjects to be virtuous; many instances of poverty, because no sufficient efforts accommodated to minds contracted by slavery, and deprived of early education have been made, to teach them how to husband their hard earnings, and to secure to themselves comfort.[6]

In short, the editors expressed the need for blacks to speak for themselves and to acquire a sense of dignity, while dis-

---

[5]See also, for example, Kessler, 28.

[6]*Freedom's Journal*, 16 March 1827.

pelling previous misrepresentations of the race based on the unconscionable actions committed by a few individuals. The editors emphasized the necessity for teaching blacks the things of which slavery, poverty, and prejudice had deprived them.

Cornish and Russwurm also planned to address the problem of educating the black population—not only basic reading and writing, but training in certain labor skills. Education, they declared, was the basis for blacks' social development.

> Education being an object of the highest importance to the welfare of society, we shall endeavor to present just and adequate views of it, and to urge upon our brethren the necessity and expediency of training their children, while young, to habits of industry, and thus forming them for becoming useful members of society.[7]

Not only did the *Journal* editors print articles and speeches on the merits of education, but Cornish occasionally published a list of African Free Schools founded by black and white abolitionists. He also criticized the teaching facilities and the lack of qualifications of the teachers. The opportunities for acquiring an education were more favorable for blacks than whites, Cornish wrote, and free blacks should raise their voices in protest.[8]

The issue presumed by some historians to be of the greatest significance, slavery, was not addressed as vehemently as education. In the original statement of purpose, the editors did not mention slavery until the latter part of the editorial.

---

[7]Ibid.

[8]*Freedom's Journal*, 1 June 1827.

Cornish and Russwurm asserted that it was the duty of *Freedom's Journal* to "vindicate our brethren, when oppressed; and to lay the case before the publick." But as for vowing any specific action against slavery, the editors were vague in their intentions. They wrote:

And while these important subjects shall occupy the columns of the FREEDOM's JOURNAL, we would not be unmindful of our brethren who are still in the iron fetters of bondage. They are our kindred by all the times of nature; and though but little can be effected by us, still let our sympathies be poured forth, and our prayers in their behalf, ascend to Him who is able to succour them.[9]

These were not staunch words that indicated a devotion to abolishing slavery. However, the intensity of the editors' stand against slavery gradually strengthened. Theodore Wright, a young abolitionist who would later work alongside Cornish, pointed out the impact created by *Freedom's Journal* in an address to the Convention of the New York State Anti-Slavery Society in 1837. According to Wright, blacks noted indications that "coercive measures" would be adopted by whites to halt black advancement.

Immediately after the insurrection in Virginia, under Nat Turner, we saw colonization spreading all over the land; and it was popular to say the people of color must be removed. The [white] press came out against us, and we trembled....Ah, Mr. President, that was a dark and gloomy period. The united views and intentions of the people of color were made known, and the nation awoke as from slumber. The *Freedom's Journal*, edited by Rev.

---

[9]*Freedom's Journal*, 16 March 1827.

Sam'l Cornish, announced the facts of the case, our entire opposition. Sir, it came like a clap of thunder.[10]

Cornish mainly limited his attacks on slavery to the columns of his newspaper and an occasional sermon. His words were cautious and subtle. Scathing sarcasm, however, also served a purpose. This characteristic is illustrated in the following excerpt from an April 6, 1827, issue: "Blessings of Slavery! Mr. John Hamilton of Lanesborough County, Va., was murdered on the 9th ult. by his slaves. Seventeen of them have been committed to the county jail to await their trial."

Despite the article mentioned above, the paper was primarily concerned with conditions in the North. However, it did occasionally include rare reports from the South—such as the first known newspaper account of a lynching.[11] The incident, which occurred on June 20, 1827, in Tuscaloosa, Alabama, appeared in the August 3 issue. The report not only included details of the crime, but emphasized that this was "the second negro who has been put to death, without Judge or Jury in that county."

Initially, Cornish edited *Freedom's Journal*, while Russwurm served as proprietor. Under Cornish's guidance, the paper flourished. Editorials were well written, and the articles provided much-needed information to aid black progress. Also, the attacks on the American Colonization Society were particularly vicious.

---

[10]Quoted in Carter Godwin Woodson, *Negro Orators and Their Orations* (New York: Russell and Russell, 1969).

[11]Charles W. Porter, "The Black Press in America Before Emancipation" (M.A. thesis, University of Alabama, Tuscaloosa, Ala., 1970), 10.

It was this last topic that might have caused the split between the two editors six months after the newspaper's inception. The issue involved the question of whether blacks would ever be free and equal to whites in the United States. Those who believed this situation would never exist advocated a colony of free blacks, chosen either voluntarily or by force, living in Africa as part of their own society. Both editors had originally been opposed to colonization. Within the first six months of operation, Russwurm began to favor the idea of colonization, while Cornish remained opposed to it.

Under Cornish's editorship, *Freedom's Journal* printed several letters from black and white readers against colonization.[12] Cornish also stated his paper's position in reply to an editorial which appeared in the Georgetown *Columbian and District Advertiser*. In the June 8, 1827, issue, Cornish wrote:

> That we have made any effort, through this Journal, to prejudice the minds of our brethren against the [American Colonization] Society, or render them suspicious of its motives, we positively deny: but that we are opposed to colonization in PRINCIPLE, OBJECT, AND TENDENCY, we, as unhesitatingly affirm. We have never desired to conceal our sentiments.

Historians disagree as to the importance of this discord between Russwurm and Cornish in their eventual breakup.[13] On September 14, 1827, Cornish announced his

---

[12]See, for example, the letter by "A Free Colored Virginian," *Freedom's Journal*, 6 July 1827; or the letter by "Investigator," 7 September 1827.

[13]See Carter R. Bryan, "Negro Journalism in America Before Emancipation," *Journalism Monographs* 12 (September 1969): 9;

resignation in a *Freedom's Journal* article which praised Russwurm and cited health and other interests as the reasons for his departure, with no mention of their differing opinions on colonization. Cornish could not have been totally disgruntled with Russwurm, since Cornish remained listed as the paper's "General Agent" throughout *Freedom's Journal*'s existence. The *Journal* also ran advertisements for Cornish and published notices of weddings he performed.

Whatever the reason, by mid-September of 1827 Cornish had resigned from his position and returned to the Presbyterian ministry, leaving Russwurm as sole editor of the paper. Attacks on the colonization society continued, but to a less severe degree than under Cornish. Russwurm began to allot more space to colonization issues, and on September 26 he also commenced printing the minutes of the society's meetings.

Ironically, it was more than a year later before Russwurm publicly declared his change of heart. Faced with the outcry raised by *Freedom's Journal* readers over the paper's policy change, Russwurm wrote a personal editorial entitled "Our Vindication" in support of his change of philosophy. In it Russwurm accused his general readership of attempting to deny his rights of free expression. He explained his change of position, citing colonization as a more preferable alternative to a life in the United States where all avenues for advancement were blocked by the issue of race. According to Russwurm,

---

Roland Wolseley, *The Black Press, U.S.A.* (Ames: Iowa State University Press, 1971), 18; and Lionel C. Barrow, Jr., "Our Own Cause: 'Freedom's Journal' and the Beginnings of the Black Press," *Journalism History* 4 (Winter 1977-78): 121.

[A black man] may possess wealth; he may be respected; he may be learned; still all united will avail him little; after all, he is considered a being of inferior order; and always will be, as no opportunity will ever be afforded him to cultivate or call into action the talents with which an All-wise Creator may have endowed him.[14]

Russwurm saw colonization as the only solution to slavery and inequality. His dream of a civilization where a black man could live without fear of being enslaved was evidenced by his commencement address at Bowdoin College. He lauded the tenacity of the Haitian people and their ability to triumph over slavery to form a government that was equitable for all citizens—an occurrence he could not envision in the United States.[15]

In a later editorial, Russwurm implored his readers not to condemn the paper on the assumption that *Freedom's Journal* approved of the forms of prejudices exercised against blacks. Of these prejudices, he concluded,

They at present exist against us—and from the length of their existence—from the degraded light in which we have ever been held—we are bold in saying, that it will never be in our power to remove or overcome them.[16]

It is unknown whether Russwurm was forced to leave the

---

[14]*Freedom's Journal*, 7 March 1829.

[15]John Browne Russwurm, "The Conditions and Prospects of Hayti," Commencement Address, Bowdoin College, 6 September 1826.

[16]*Freedom's Journal*, 14 March 1829.

paper because of his conversion to colonization or if his fervor for the cause led to his resignation. He soon gave up his position on the paper and moved to a colony in Liberia. He went on to become the superintendent of public schools and later the editor of the *Liberia Herald.* He concluded his editorial duties at *Freedom's Journal* with his March 28, 1829, column. In it, he declared that he was "not the least astonished, that we have been slandered by the villainous—that our name is [a] byword among the more ignorant, for what could we expect?" He also listed what he considered to have been the original objectives of *Freedom's Journal,* which included: "the dissemination of useful knowledge; the defence [sic] of our community; the necessity and advantages of education; and lately, the expediency of emigration to Liberia."

When Russwurm departed for Liberia, Cornish returned to *Freedom's Journal* as editor—changing the name to the *Rights of All.* However, the paper's purposes remained the same—to provide accurate representation of blacks; to promote the advantages of diligence and economy; to extol the virtues of good moral character; and to instill within the readers the importance of education in improving the circumstances of their day-to-day existence.[17]

Cornish himself served as an example to the black community. He had risen from extreme poverty to relatively prosperous respectability, and he maintained an intellectual commitment to the idea that the race would have to do likewise.[18] He believed that blacks' failure to prosper economically and to acquire the skills to do so was the result of a ten-

---

[17]*Rights of All,* 29 May 1829.

[18]Jane H. Pease and William H. Pease, *They Who Would Be Free: Blacks' Search for Freedom, 1830-1861* (New York: Atheneum, 1974), 262.

dency to "grasp after flowers, and neglect solid and wholesome fruits."[19]

Cornish never lost the opportunity to instill in his readers the need for education. He believed that through education blacks could help abolish prejudice and advance through the social ranks. *Freedom's Journal* and *Rights of All* encouraged education for blacks by advertising private schools in New York City and elsewhere and by promoting interest in the city's African Free Schools, organized and run by the New York Manumission Society. When the African Free Schools were hindered by declining attendance, Cornish established visiting committees to urge parents to send their children to school. Meanwhile, a committee was also formed to sew for children who lacked sufficient clothing to attend classes. Progress of both committee groups was duly reported in *Freedom's Journal*.[20]

Upon his return to the paper, Cornish also wasted no time in renewing his attacks against the colonizationists. His June 12, 1829, editorial declared that the goal of returning the "sons of Africa" to her coasts was a trifling matter, and the important tasks were to educate blacks and encourage them to pursue agricultural and mechanical careers. Cornish's editorial also stated,

That the interest of the christian public, in behalf of the coloured people of this country, has diminished, in proportion to their zeal, in behalf of the Liberian colony, is evident to every enlightened man of colour, and also to every unprejudiced white man, and it is not our duty to call back,

---

[19]*Rights of All*, 18 September 1829.

[20]See, for example, *Freedom's Journal*, 21 December 1827; 11 January 1828; and 1 February 1828.

or at least to call for a division of the public attention, the public effort, and the public prayers in behalf of our brethren in this country.[21]

His idea of an industrious black race coincided with the paper's original philosophy for improving the black way of life, which encouraged blacks to learn a trade and to channel it into economically productive undertakings. *Freedom's Journal* readers had always been warned to buy only necessities, to save against hard times, and to invest surplus income carefully.[22]

Another of Cornish's causes expressed in the pages of the *Rights of All* was promoting responsible voting practices by qualified blacks who did not exercise the privileges. Since many free states barred most free blacks from voting by using such techniques as qualification tests and intimidation, Cornish thought it the duty of those who qualified to participate in New York elections. Not only did he urge the people to vote, but he chastised the "State" for using qualification tests that applied only to blacks.[23]

After Russwurm's departure, Cornish had hoped to revive the paper's sagging circulation figures and restore it to its former place as a leader of the black community. Russwurm's change of position on the colonization issue had alienated many of the paper's former supporters, leading to a reduction in subscribers. Abolitionist David Walker, whose pamphlet aimed toward the black population was the first sustained written assault upon U.S. slavery and racism,

---

[21]*Rights of All*, 12 June 1829.

[22]See, for example, *Freedom's Journal*, 30 May 1828.

[23]See *Rights of All*, 16 October 1829.

was a strong supporter of Cornish and the *Rights of All*. He appealed to blacks for their "cordial co-operation in the circulation of 'The Rights of All,' among us. The utility of such a vehicle if rightly conducted, cannot be estimated....I believe he [Cornish] is not seeking to fill his pockets with money, but has the welfare of his brethren truly at heart."[24]

Despite Cornish's continued emphasis on the need for a means of communication between black Americans, a lack of financial support by the latter part of 1829 forced him to give up his efforts. Starved for subscriptions despite efforts of stockholders and friends to save it, the *Rights of All* (formerly *Freedom's Journal*) ceased publication.

Although short-lived, the paper had served to incite blacks into action and then recorded the results. However, its motive was not to instigate concerted action against slavery. Items pertaining to slavery, such as the editorial appearing on October 17, 1828, were extremely rare. The justification for that editorial was probably the proximity of the episode it addressed. The wharf from which a boat loaded with slaves departed for North Carolina or Virginia for later reshipping to New Orleans was located in New York City.[25] Because of the location, Cornish deemed the event significant and worthy of editorial comment. Previous articles on slavery-related issues had been on events farther away, but this incident brought the issue to the Northern free blacks' own backyard.

On the contrary, the editors themselves made bigger statements about antislavery than their newspaper. Russ-

---

[24]David Walker, *Walker's Appeal, in Four Articles; Together with a Preamble, to the Colored Citizens of the World* (Boston: By the author, 1830).

[25]*Freedom's Journal*, 17 October 1828.

wurm's departure incurred the displeasure of many of his former friends. In 1831, his successful editorship at the *Liberia Herald* and his increased political activity in Africa sparked a series of letters from outraged former supporters in the United States. One letter to the editor of the *Liberator* from a writer designated only as "R." declared that Russwurm's "ingratitude" would never be obliterated from the minds of his followers. He accused Russwurm of subverting the "pledge he made to colored brethren" and leaving the country "to dwell in that land for which the temptor MONEY caused him to avow his preferment."[26] Another letter writer, "C.D.T., a Philadelphian," also attributed Russwurm's change of attitude toward colonization to monetary gain. The writer determined that Russwurm converted the paper into a tool of the colonization society after failing to gain enough subscribers to support it.[27]

Russwurm's support of colonization also reduced his popularity among leaders of the period. With the exception of black leader and fellow journalist Martin Robison Delany, who praised Russwurm as an exemplary scholar, businessman, and community leader,[28] black leaders of the nineteenth century never forgave Russwurm for his alleged defection. Believing that a return to Africa and a revival of the great empires of the Middle Ages were the only escape for the black man, Russwurm expressed these ideas frequently during the time prior to his resignation. Other things which

---

[26]*Liberator*, 16 April 1831.

[27]*Liberator*, 30 April 1831.

[28]Martin Robison Delany, *The Condition, Elevation, Emigration, and Destiny of the Colored People of the United States* (Philadelphia: By the author, 1852), 129.

angered blacks in the community, who often burned him in effigy, were Russwurm's acceptance of an offer to join the Maryland Colonization Society and his defense of black exclusion laws in Ohio—both of which encouraged the emigration back to Africa. By supporting these ideas in *Freedom's Journal*, he was accused of "selling out" to the enemies of the black people.[29]

Yet Delany saw Russwurm as a "gentleman of splendid talents" who "as his first public act, commenced the publication of a newspaper, for the elevation of colored Americans, called '*Freedom's Journal*.'"[30] In his book, *The Condition, Elevation, Emigration, and Destiny of the Colored People of the United States*, Delany failed to mention Cornish as a collaborator for the paper or the uproar caused by Russwurm's colonization beliefs.

During the nineteenth century, leaders, unlike Delany, were almost unanimous in their denunciation of Russwurm and praise for Cornish. Today, Cornish is virtually forgotten, while Russwurm is considered a noted black nationalist.[31]

While attitudes toward Russwurm became increasingly negative, Cornish continued to maintain a respected position in the black community. His sermons were of especial significance to abolitionist William Lloyd Garrison. In a letter to his future wife, Helen Benson, Garrison detailed his attendance at sermons by Cornish and the Rev. Peter Williams and how he had "taken by the hand many of my colored friends, who were overjoyed to see me. To-morrow

---

[29]Bennett, 65.

[30]Delany, 129.

[31]Bennett, 65.

evening I shall meet some of the leading colored gentlemen, in relation to future concerns of the *Liberator* [Garrison's abolitionist newspaper]."[32]

Cornish also collaborated closely with ministers Williams and Theodore Wright and abolitionist Arthur Tappan in organizing the New York City Anti-Slavery Society. However, Cornish and the others became the society's sharpest critics—objecting to the low priority given to expanding black rights and job opportunities and to the white organizers' patronizing paternalism.

Consequently, Cornish never terminated his battle for equal rights and a higher social status for blacks. He applied his original principles to the operation and purpose of his second newspaper, the *Colored American*. He also became an active member in the national Negro conventions, which were politically oriented gatherings of black leaders that stressed the importance of advancements in black rights.

The task the two men began with *Freedom's Journal*—to create a newspaper that would fulfill the needs of the black society in America—was taken up by many others, both black and white. Whatever they sought to accomplish, Cornish and Russwurm had no way of knowing that their journalistic endeavors would be imitated and would multiply, despite immense hardships. *Freedom's Journal* was the black response to a closed forum for expression in the conventional press, and it labored through a period of high illiteracy among blacks and low circulation figures. Freedom and civility toward blacks dominated the pages of the paper, but *Freedom's Journal* was the first stage of a crusade for a black newspaper that would suit the informational needs of a black community.

---

[32]William Lloyd Garrison to Helen Benson, ALS, April 1834, Villard Papers, Harvard College Library, Cambridge.

2

THE *WEEKLY ADVOCATE* AND THE *COLORED AMERICAN*: THE SEARCH FOR UNITY

Financial difficulties and a lack of community support contributed to the failure of the majority of early black newspapers, leaving New York blacks virtually with no medium for voicing their opinions or receiving information tailored to their specific needs. More than seven years elapsed between the termination of *Freedom's Journal* and the creation of the *Colored American*, normally considered to be the second oldest black newspaper based on its longevity and community influence. After *Freedom's Journal* ceased publication, blacks were left without a newspaper devoted especially to their needs. At first, free northern blacks supported William Lloyd Garrison's *Liberator*.[1] Since, however, the *Liberator* was dedicated to expressing the Garrisonian philosophies, it had little room to devote to items of specific interest to blacks.

---

[1]Donald M. Jacobs, "William Lloyd Garrison's *Liberator* and Boston's Blacks, 1830-1865," *New England Quarterly* 44 (June 1971): 259-277.

Another proposal for a paper under the title of *The African Sentinel and Journal of Liberty* appeared in the *Liberator* on March 12, 1831. Established in Albany, N.Y., the paper was edited by John E. Stewart. He declared that the paper was for the "general advancement and improvement of the people of color." He lamented the failure of *Freedom's Journal* despite the efforts of Samuel Cornish and vowed to fill the void with his new publication. Unfortunately, the prospectus for the paper was dated January 26, 1831, and only four monthly papers appeared through August 1831. No copy of the paper has been found.[2] A checklist of Negro newspapers published before emancipation includes two other newspapers that originated before the *Weekly Advocate*: the *Spirit of the Times*, published in New York City, 1836-1842, which failed to produce a large following, and *The National Reformer* in Philadelphia, a short-lived paper published in 1833.[3] It was not until 1837 that blacks conceived a paper which would earn the reputation of the earlier *Freedom's Journal.*

Founded by Phillip A. Bell in January of 1837, the *Colored American* was originally named the *Weekly Advocate*. Like Samuel Cornish and John Russwurm of *Freedom's Journal*, Bell had no journalistic experience. He was one of New York City's leading black businessmen, operating an office which aided blacks in locating domestic positions.[4] However, he was well respected by both blacks and

---

[2]Herbert Aptheker, ed., *A Documentary History of the Negro People in the United States* (New York: The Citadel, 1951), 109-110.

[3]Carter R. Bryan, "Negro Journalism in America Before Emancipation," *Journalism Monographs* 12 (September 1969): 30.

[4]Martin R. Delany, *The Condition, Elevation, Emigration, and Destiny of the Colored People of the United States* (Philadelphia: By

whites in the community, and his paper was well received. The paper was to be an "advocate" of the members of the black community. According to the *Advocate's* statement of purpose,

> The people of color have often said among themselves, We want an Advocate of our own—devoted particularly to our own interests—conducted by ourselves, devoted to our moral, mental and political improvement, containing the news of the day, and a variety of scientific and literary matter; and ONE in which we can make known our various and respective occupations in life, through the medium of advertising. To such we say, Look here! Today you have spread before your eyes the desideratum you have so long, and ardently prayed for. Here is your ADVOCATE and FRIEND....[5]

Like its predecessor, *Freedom's Journal*, the *Weekly Advocate* was a forum for the black voices of the period. As illustrated in the statement of purpose, the editors sought the opportunity to speak for blacks and to express blacks' position on a variety of issues. Among those subjects was also dedication to establishing a place for blacks in America's mainstream society—a cause which the paper supported vehemently from the very beginning. One part of that goal was to develop a society where free blacks received all the rights available to their white counterparts. In the paper's second issue, January 14, 1837, the editors challenged the appropriateness of using the term "free man" when blacks were being deprived of many of their civil rights. In short, the term was a mockery "when [blacks were] so unrighteously de-

---

the author, 1852), 103.

[5]"Our Undertaking," *Weekly Advocate*, 7 January 1837.

prived of every civil and political privilege....When almost every honorable incentive to the pursuit of happiness, so largely and so freely held out to his fairer brother, is withheld from him."[6] The editorial lashed out against racial prejudice and the resulting restrictions that barred blacks from lucrative employment, a formal education, and access to various public recreational facilities. However, there seemed to be a sense of hope offered near the end of the editorial—a shared goal for which all blacks could strive. The editorial concluded,

We trust, however, that the day is not far distant when oppression and prejudice will cease their unhallowed war, against the innocent and unoffending, and that every man of colour will not only nominally, but in reality, enjoy all the blessings and privileges of free men, native AMERICAN FREE MEN."[7]

The term "American" would become a key component in the paper's quest for black citizens' rights. Its importance became evident when the name of the *Weekly Advocate* was changed to indicate the emphasis on blacks' demands for full citizenship rights. Two months after its founding, the paper was renamed the *Colored American*, and Samuel Cornish was obtained as editor. Bell and Cornish had both been members of the first National Negro Convention in 1830, which was formed to address issues of major concern to American blacks. Cornish was described by his peers as the man "who had the distinguished honor of reasoning Gerrit Smith out of colonizationism, and of telling Henry Clay that

---

[6]*Weekly Advocate*, 14 January 1837.

[7]Ibid.

he would never be president of anything higher than the American Colonization Society," while Bell was "the born *sabreur* who never feared the face of clay."[8] After his appointment by Bell, Cornish completed one of his first duties as *Colored American* editor—explaining the reasons for selecting the new name. According to Cornish,

> In complexion, in blood and in nativity, we are decidedly more exclusively 'American' than our white brethren; hence the propriety of the name of our paper, *Colored American*, and of identifying the name with all our institutions, in spite of our enemies, who would rob us of our nationality and reproach us as exoticks [sic].[9]

Cornish reasoned that "Colored American" was inoffensive and more acceptable to use in unifying the black community than other terms such as Negroes, Africans, and blacks. With a name devoid of reproach, the paper, under Cornish's direction, was to "carry to him [every man] lessons of instruction on religion and morals, lessons on industry and economy—until our entire people are of one heart and of one mind, in all the means of their salvation, both temporal and spiritual."[10]

Cornish urged his readers to support the paper so that blacks scattered in communities throughout the North could

---

[8]Interview with Hezekiah Grice, quoted in *The Anglo-American*, October 1859.

[9]"Proposals and Plan of a Newspaper of Color," *Colored American*, 4 March 1837.

[10]Ibid.

be drawn together and changes effected.[11] The *Colored American* served as an information center for the black population in New York City. It was originally subsidized by abolitionist Arthur Tappan.[12] Yet, financing for the paper in its later months of operation was precarious, despite funds generated by the $1.50 per year in advance subscription rate. The executive committee of the American Anti-Slavery Society endorsed the paper for its members and at the annual meeting in 1838 encouraged members to subscribe.[13] Other organizations such as the New York State Anti-Slavery Society and the Massachusetts Female Emancipation Society also took up collections for the weekly paper. The antislavery society president, Gerrit Smith, voiced his support by sending Cornish a personal donation of $10 and a letter on August 22, 1837, which included the statement, "I must occasionally send you a few dollars toward sustaining your excellent paper. The Lord bless you."[14]

Despite financial worries, the paper operated for four years, completing many of the objectives established by its editors. As evidenced by its financial supporters, the *Colored American* maintained strong connections with antislavery activists. Yet, in addition to recording antislavery activities of Northern blacks, the 11-by-16-inch, four-page, four-column paper also included items on the importance of indus-

---

[11]*Colored American*, 18 March 1837.

[12]Lewis Tappan, *Life of Arthur Tappan* (New York: Hurd and Houghton, 1870), 185.

[13]*Minutes of the Pennsylvania Society for Promoting the Abolition of Slavery (1827-1847)* (Philadelphia: Historical Society of Pennsylvania, n.d.).

[14]*Colored American*, 2 September 1837.

triousness, culture, morality, education, and suffrage.

Cornish had always considered self-help to be an important part in the elevation and refinement of blacks. Therefore, industriousness and diligence were encouraged often in the columns of the *Colored American*. Through work, each "one for himself, must commence the improvement of his condition. It is not in mass, but in individual effort and character, that we are to move onward to a higher elevation."[15] However, certain criteria had to be met. Before blacks could take their rightful place in society, they had to make several crucial changes. First, blacks were to abandon former useless practices and "cultivate honesty, punctuality, propriety of conduct, and modesty and dignity of deportment." Second, they were to engage in "untiring habits of industry, the dint of perseverance." Third, money was not to be spent on improving outward appearance, but "for the purpose of elevating our character, and improving our condition." Finally, blacks were to cultivate their intellect through the "accumulation of knowledge, extensive and solid."[16] The *Colored American* also became part of a larger campaign to help channel black energies toward more productive undertakings. Cornish explained that lotteries were usually rigged in favor of the operators and were also illegal and poor investments. Time could be better spent reading, attending lectures, and improving the mind.[17]

Despite emphasizing individual assiduity, the *Colored American* also stressed the necessity of cooperation and unity within the black community, as well as the need for a

---

[15]*Colored American*, 22 April 1837.

[16]*Colored American*, 6 May 1837.

[17]See *Colored American*, 23 February 1839; and 18 March 1837.

concerted effort to educate the black population as a means of ensuring the future of the race. A September 1, 1838, issue supported the idea that "in the youth among us, we look to see our people brought forward and incorporated in all the ramifications of society. In them are our clerks, and merchants and mechanics, and farmers, and manufacturers."[18]

Cornish again revived his campaign for the education of blacks, both young and old. Through education, blacks could earn an equal position in American society. According to Cornish, education was not only a means of advancement, but it was an opportunity to prevent immoral activities. Cornish wrote:

There are three thousand children among us, out of school; not only losing the advantages of a good education, but growing up in idleness, and without that moral restraint which a good school exercises over its scholars....Our infant sons, should we give them suitable advantages, will be as eligible to the Presidency of the United States, as any other portions of the community; and it is our wisdom, if possible, to give them as ample qualifications.[19]

To further those aims, the *Colored American* was a strong proponent of black suffrage and political involvement. Editors encouraged black readers to exercise the few political rights they possessed to address a variety of issues. A March 4, 1837, editorial by then general correspondent Charles Bennett Ray, "On the Right of Colored People to Vote," proclaimed:

---

[18]*Colored American*, 1 September 1838.

[19]*Colored American*, 1 July 1837.

For the last fifteen years the exercise of this right [suffrage] has been denied to all colored male citizens, except those who own a freehold estate of $250 in value: a provision by which all but a mere fraction of the 44,000 people of this state have been disfranchised.[20]

Earlier in the year Cornish had coordinated a petition campaign to repeal this constitutional provision for black voters. Bell, the *Colored American*'s publisher, and Ray, already a well-established clergyman, worked as campaign coordinators at the New York City headquarters.[21] The following year New York City blacks created the Association for the Political Elevation and Improvement of the People of Color, while the *Colored American* continued to urge blacks to press further in the franchise issue.[22]

In other issues of the *Colored American*, blacks were also urged to speak out on the admission of states to the Union as "free" or "slave." The paper also advocated utilizing black political power with the possibility of reforming voting restrictions and urged black voters to form a new party when existing political parties proved unresponsive.[23]

It was this unresponsiveness by white political and community leaders on other key issues that led *Colored*

---

[20]*Colored American*, 4 March 1837.

[21]Emil Olbrich, *The Development of Sentiment on Negro Suffrage to 1860*, Bulletin of the University of Wisconsin, 477, History Series, Vol. 3, no. 1 (Madison: University of Wisconsin, 1921), 35-36. See also *Colored American*, 11 March 1837; and 19 August 1837.

[22]*Colored American*, 16 June 1838.

[23]See, for example, *Colored American*, 6 May 1837; 3 September 1837; and 10 October 1840.

American editors to oppose colonization and slavery from the paper's outset. Both Bell and Cornish were already firm opponents of colonization. Bell had denounced colonization and the American Colonization Society at a mass meeting of blacks in New York City on January 25, 1831.[24] Cornish, who had opposed colonization since before his partnership with John Russwurm in *Freedom's Journal*, continued his campaign in the *Colored American*. To those supporting colonization, Cornish declared "we would rather die a thousand deaths, in *honestly* and *legally* contending for our rights *in this our native country*....We will stay and seek the purification of the whole lump."[25]

This determination to remain and improve the current situation resulted in the editors' indirect attacks on slavery. The editors approached this objective in a variety of ways. Warnings about kidnappers in town or arrests of free men as fugitive slaves appeared regularly, as well as articles exhorting the lack of racial unity as a primary cause of slavery.[26] In the following article, the intended kidnap victim was not only warned of the danger, but was informed of a possible escape route:

"LOOK OUT FOR KIDNAPPERS!"

A woman had been "accosted" by two men from Georgia, who tried to abduct her as they believed she was an escaped slave. If there be any such a woman in New York, this notice is to warn her to escape to the mountains, and remain

---

[24]*Liberator*, 12 February 1831.

[25]*Colored American*, 30 September 1837.

[26]See, for example, *Colored American*, 6 February 1841; 16 January 1841; and 27 January 1838.

there until the Georgia and New York kidnappers shall have been consumed by the mighty spirit of liberty.[27]

Slavery was only one of many issues on which the editors of the *Colored American* focused. The variety of topics addressed reflected their personal interests and concerns. Ironically, these pursuits, and enlarged financial burdens, eventually lured them away from their positions at the *Colored American*. In June 1837 the paper had only nine hundred subscribers and was operating in the red.[28] It was also saddled with a fine and court costs when John Russell, a landlord for Negro seamen, filed a libel suit over activist David Ruggles' exposé of illegal slave trading. Lewis and Arthur Tappan, Gerrit Smith, William Jay, James G. Birney, and others came to the paper's rescue with funds, and the earlier endorsement by the antislavery society and the female emancipation group had also brought some relief.[29] In 1838, though, a second reorganization was needed. Cornish had not been paid since 1837 and was eager to turn much of the editorial burden over to James McCune Smith, a practicing physician and lecturer who frequently contributed editorials to the paper. By the summer of 1839, Cornish retired as editor to resume his clerical duties and his community activities with such organizations as the New York Committee of Vigilance and the National Negro Convention. Smith took over some of the editorial duties, while

---

[27]*Colored American*, 4 April 1840.

[28]Jane H. Pease and William H. Pease, *They Who Would Be Free: Blacks' Search for Freedom, 1830-1861* (New York: Atheneum, 1974), 114.

[29]Ibid., 210-211.

the Rev. Charles Bennett Ray succeeded Bell as proprietor. Ray, pastor of the Bethesda Congregational Church, was first associated with the paper as a general agent or correspondent in 1837, while Bell was still proprietor and editorial writer. In 1838 Ray had taken over most of Bell's proprietorial duties, and by 1839 Bell relinquished his editorship as well. He continued with his business in New York for many years before moving to California and establishing another newspaper, *The Elevator*, in 1865 in San Francisco.[30] The *Colored American* suspended publication until March 7, 1840, when Ray assumed both positions as editor and proprietor.[31]

Ray continued many of the practices begun by Bell and Cornish and also expanded the paper into other areas. Ray intended to make it "a first-rate family paper, devoting a column to the instruction of children, giving the general news of the day...and nothing of an immoral tendency can find a place in its columns."[32] Ray sought readers in both the white and black communities. For the whites, the paper was to offer the opportunity for them to become acquainted with the black viewpoint, while he felt that the blacks owed the paper their aid in advancing their causes.[33] Ray had a reputation as a fighter, and he wanted to make the *Colored American* into a paper "that will be known for ages as a bold and uncompromising fighter for freedom."[34] He shared

---

[30]See, for example, Pease and Pease, 114; and Bryan, 13.

[31]Bryan, 13.

[32]Irving Garland Penn, *The Afro-American Press and Its Editors* (Springfield, Mass.: Wiley and Co., 1891), 38.

[33]Ibid., 39.

Cornish's sentiments about such topics as the importance of education, diligence, and suffrage. He also maintained the paper's advocacy of black unity and racial justice, but he disagreed with Cornish on many points. For example, he felt that Cornish had been lax in many of his duties, and he set about remedying the oversights. While Cornish had stressed the importance of moral development, Ray believed that he had overlooked the most obvious group of blacks who needed the instruction, the children. Ray created a regular column, "Youth Department," devoted to the moral instruction and direction of children. Articles in the form of narratives or parables encouraged the practice of a strict set of values. Like Cornish, Ray also promoted the need for blacks to organize and operate for the good of all.

However, while Cornish advocated identifying all people as Americans with similar interests, Ray supported the idea that "there are and will be special interests for us [blacks] to attend to, so long as American caste exists, and we have not equal rights, in common with the American people."[35] This position led to a distinctive clash between Cornish and Ray. Cornish believed that one political group could ideally represent the interests of both black and white abolitionists, while Ray promoted the use of exclusive race conventions to create a black political faction devoted especially to serve the needs of blacks in individual states. Thus, race became an issue among abolitionists, leading to separate conventions and a split among abolitionist groups. Political activity was only one of many disagreements which led to this split among abolitionists. Disputes also centered around female equality and the denunciation of all established churches, an issue supported strongly by

---

[34]Ibid., 46.

[35]*Colored American*, 2 May 1840.

William Lloyd Garrison. The white abolitionist group divided into the American Anti-Slavery Society and the newly created Foreign Anti-Slavery Society. The Negro abolitionists also split, with such men as William C. Nell, James G. Barbadoes, and William P. Powell supporting Garrison, and Samuel Cornish, Christopher Rush, and Charles Ray functioning as members of the first executive committee of the new organization.[36]

Ray filled the columns of the *Colored American* with reports of this debate, particularly matters relating to political activity. Gerrit Smith and the New York Anti-Slavery Society refused to continue endorsing the paper until it changed its course on politics. Antislavery feuding was beginning to destroy the paper's original objectives of establishing black unity.

Ultimately, the *Colored American* failed to generate the enthusiasm and support necessary from the community it served in order to survive. It finally ceased publication in 1841.[37] Apparently, an edition of the *Colored American* had also been printed for readers in Philadelphia from 1838 to 1841. It is also believed to have ended at the same time.

Like *Freedom's Journal*, the *Colored American* had not limited its focus to slavery. It served as a local bulletin for blacks in New York City and the surrounding community, recording antislavery activities on a state and national level and providing insight into suffrage rights, morality, and education. Its circulation peaked at more than 2,000 in northern states from Maine to Michigan and had reached a

---

[36]Aptheker, 192.

[37]Some historians, such as Bryan, believe it did not end until 1842, but the theory has not been substantiated. Microfilm only exists up to March 1841.

larger and more sophisticated readership than *Freedom's Journal.*

The failure of the *Colored American*, like that of other black newspapers of the period, cannot be attributed solely to the editors and publishers. Perhaps the poverty of the potential subscribers and inadequate financial resources were also contributing factors. The lack of success was no indication of an absence of will or determination. The influence and importance of the *Colored American* and other early black newspapers are illustrated by the following excerpt from *The Herald of Freedom*, a white abolitionist paper in Concord, N.H.:

> It is no longer necessary for abolitionists to contend against the blunder of pro-slavery, —that the colored people are inferior to the whites; for these people are practically demonstrating its falseness. They have enough men of action now, to maintain the anti-slavery enterprise, and to win their liberty, and that of their enslaved brethren—if every white abolitionist were drawn from the field: McCune Smith, and Cornish, and [Theodore] Wright and Ray and a host of others....The people of such men as these cannot be held in slavery. They have got their pens drawn, and their voices, and they are seen to be the pens and voices of human genius; and they will neither lay down the one nor will they hush the other, till their brethren are free.[38]

The *Colored American* represented the next stage in the development of a black press that would become a major medium of communication for the race. It served not only as their spokesman, but also as their teacher and the chronicler of an integral part of American history.

---

[38]Penn, 40.

3

THE RAM'S HORN:
A VOICE FOR BLACKS

Although slavery continued to be an important topic of the period as evidenced by earlier black newspapers such as *Freedom's Journal* and the *Colored American*, it had little direct influence on establishing another black-owned newspaper in New York. Discriminatory voting requirements for blacks indirectly led to the creation of the New York City newspaper, *The Ram's Horn*. A clause in the state constitution provided voting privileges for blacks in New York only if they owned $250 in real estate with all taxes paid. By comparison, any white man at least 20 years of age could vote, regardless of land ownership.[1]

A public campaign in 1846 sought to change the clause by popular vote, while the New York *Sun* continued to advocate a vote of "no."[2] Willis A. Hodges, a black businessman,

---

[1]I. Garland Penn, *The Afro-American Press and Its Editors* (Springfield, Mass.: Wiley and Co., 1891), 61.

[2]Equal suffrage was an issue of major concern with New Yorkers in 1845. The state legislature submitted to popular referendum an act to remove the special property qualification imposed on black voters. The referendum was defeated, but the constitutional convention

initiated a campaign to win approval for the amendment despite the *Sun's* opposition. Hodges wrote that the *Sun* had biased white voters against the campaign "by telling them if they wanted to have a 'nigger' marry into their families and many other objectionable things...to vote 'yes,' if not, to vote 'no.'"[3] Hodges prepared a response to the *Sun's* editorials, but was refused publication until he paid $15. The *Sun* then treated Hodges' article as a paid advertisement and placed it in an obscure corner of the paper. When Hodges protested, an editor told him that "'the *Sun* shines for all white men, not black men. You must get up a paper of your own if you want to tell your side of the story to the public.'"[4]

Hodges had no idea of the skills, equipment, funding, and other necessities required in operating a newspaper. A farmer originally from Princess Anne County, Virginia, he operated a stall in the Catharine Market near New York's Catharine Slip, where he sold produce, chickens, and ducks.[5] However, prompted by the editor's words and the growing need for a black journal in New York—previous black-owned publications had ceased operation usually

---

placed an equal suffrage amendment before the voters in 1846. For examples of editorials opposing equal suffrage for blacks, see New York *Sun*, 1 November 1845-1 June 1846.

[3]Willard B. Gatewood, Jr., ed., *Free Man of Color: The Autobiography of Willis Augustus Hodges* (Knoxville: University of Tennessee Press, 1982), 75-76. Hodges intended that his autobiography, completed in 1849, be published in behalf of the free people of color of the times. However, it was not until his death that his son Augustus serialized the autobiography in the weekly Indianapolis *Freeman* for seven consecutive months, beginning in March 1896. This later version remains as it appeared in the *Freeman*.

[4]Ibid., 76.

[5]Gatewood, xxxvii.

within less than a year—Hodges set out to gain support for his project. Few blacks were eager to invest in a black newspaper after observing so many others collapse under financial pressures. He finally approached Thomas Van Rensselaer, an old friend and well-known restauranteur. Van Rensselaer had run away from his master in Mohawk Valley in New York in 1819 and ultimately established a restaurant in New York. He was a well-known black abolitionist in the 1830s and 1840s and had welcomed William Lloyd Garrison as a guest in his home in 1840.[6] Van Rensselaer agreed to join Hodges in the venture if Hodges could raise the money to begin the business. Hodges earned the money doing whitewashing jobs throughout New York City six days a week.[7] In a later interview with historian Irving Garland Penn, Hodges recalled how he had saved enough money after two months of work, "...and I can truly say that I furnished every dollar that started *The Ram's Horn*, and wrote the first article that was published in its columns."[8]

On January 1, 1847, Hodges and Van Rensselaer, who served as the paper's business manager, released their first edition of *The Ram's Horn*. Hodges chose the name from a passage in Joshua (6:5):

And it shall come to pass that when they make a loud blast with the ram's horn, and ye shall hear the sound of the trumpet, all the people shall shout, and the walls of the city shall fall down flat and the people shall ascend up, every

---

[6]Carleton Mabee, *Black Freedom: The Non-Violent Abolitionists from 1830 through the Civil War* (London: Macmillan, 1970), 130 and 270.

[7]Gatewood, 76-77.

[8]Penn, 63.

man straight before Him.

The paper's motto, "We are men and therefore are interested in whatever concerns men," reflected Hodges' disapproval of the *Sun* editor's response to presenting all sides of a story, regardless of race.

The prospectus for the paper, composed by Hodges, also appeared in the first edition. In it, Hodges encouraged "the people of color, both bond and free, and all the friends of freedom's cause, both white and black," to subscribe to the four-page weekly. The prospectus read in part:

We hope like Joshua of old, to blow the "Ram's Horn" (once a week) until the walls of slavery and injustice fall, and ask the good people of New York to shout with us and hold up our arms (by way of subscriptions and articles of the day) trusting that the same God that successfully fought the battle for His people in the days of old, will, in His own time and way, fight ours, and give us the victory.[9]

The subscription rate for New York City residents was $1.50 per year, three cents per copy or $1 per year in advance for mail subscribers.[10] At most gatherings of blacks in or near New York City during the eighteen months of *The Ram's Horn*'s operation, either Hodges or Van Rensselaer was present to promote the paper and to seek subscriptions and donations. At one point subscriptions to the paper reached almost 3,000.[11]

---

[9]*The Ram's Horn*, 1 January 1847.

[10]Ibid.

[11]H. Lewis Dorsey, "Progress of Afro-American Journalism," Parsons (Kan.) *Weekly Blade*, 28 April 1894.

Consisting of four pages of five columns each, the weekly received many pronouncements of support and admiration. Its articles were noted for their "readability and force of character."[12] Like its black-owned predecessors, *The Ram's Horn* addressed a variety of topics aimed at guarding "the rights and interests of an outraged race."[13] Although November 5, 1847, is the only extant issue of *The Ram's Horn*, it gives some indication of the wide range of stories addressed. The edition included items such as an editorial urging blacks to accept land in upstate New York donated by philanthropist and abolitionist Gerrit Smith for distribution to 3,000 blacks from throughout New York state; an item dealing with petitions against war with Mexico; an article on black suffrage; and others on church activities.

The November 5 issue served as a forum for one cause Hodges had advocated as a delegate to a national convention of blacks held in Troy, N. Y., on October 6-9, 1847. The major items on the agenda included "education, anti-slavery, necessity for acquiring worldly goods, promotion of temperance and frugality, and necessity of migration to the farm."[14] Hodges was particularly supportive of a banking institution for blacks and the virtues of agricultural life. He co-authored the convention's report on agriculture with Charles B. Ray, minister and former editor of the *Colored American*. According to the report, agriculture encouraged individual self-reliance, advanced "moral, mental, and

---

[12]Penn, 61-63.

[13]*The Ram's Horn*, 5 November 1847.

[14]Howard H. Bell, ed., "Proceedings of the National Convention of Colored People and their Friends, October 6-9, 1847," *Minutes of the Proceedings of the National Negro Convention, 1830-1864* (New York: Arno Press, 1969), 1-17.

physical culture," and promoted equality.[15] Hodges also sponsored resolutions, approved by the convention, expressing appreciation to Gerrit Smith for his donation of farmland for blacks. This interest in Smith's offer and the merits of an agricultural life were illustrated in the editorial on Smith appearing in the November 5, 1847, edition.[16]

Having been active in a variety of black causes and interests, Hodges and Van Rensselaer reflected these concerns in the columns of their newspaper. Hodges, who received little formal education, helped to form the New York Society for the Promotion of Education Among Colored Children, a black-controlled organization that sponsored and operated schools for black children in New York City.[17] Another of Hodges' interests was temperance and the need to rid the black population of the "great evil" of alcohol. Hodges had not only witnessed the destructive consequences of alcohol abuse, but he had also been the target for personal abuse by drunken vigilantes in Princess Anne County, Virginia. He organized the Union Temperance Benevolent Society and served as its president from 1841 until 1848.[18] He advocated both of these causes whenever he had the opportunity.

The immediate success of *The Ram's Horn* was both surprising and encouraging to Hodges and Van Rensselaer, prompting much needed support and recognition. William Lloyd Garrison's *Liberator* described it as a jour-

---

[15]Ibid.

[16]Ibid.

[17]Alexander Moore, *Nelson-Hodges Papers, 1773-1936* (New York: Long Island Historical Society, n.d.), 7-8.

[18]See, for example, Jane H. Pease and William H. Pease, *They Who Would Be Free: Blacks' Search for Freedom, 1830-1861* (New York: Atheneum, 1974), 120-22.

nal which was dedicated to "the abolition of slavery and the elevation of the colored population of the United States" and which the editors "conducted with spirit and ability."[19] *The National Anti-Slavery Standard* lauded the editors' "ability and independence," describing *The Ram's Horn* as "a handsome sheet and filled with well-selected and well-written editorial matter."[20]

One of the more notable editorials was one obviously directed to enslaved blacks in the South and voiced both Hodges' and Van Rensselaer's outspoken opposition to slavery. It was one of the few examples of written material directed toward a people considered by many to be illiterate and unintelligent. The editorial, "Slaves of the South, Now Is Your Time," exhorted the slaves to combat slavery and its accompanying tyranny. It advised slaves not "to murder the slaveholders; but we do advise you to refuse longer to work without pay. Make up your minds to die, rather than bequeath a state of slavery to your posterity." The editors also urged the men to join this cause which the world was observing in order "to see the glorious result of liberty, of equality, triumph over slavery and oppression."[21]

Hodges assumed the majority of the editorial responsibilities for the paper, with occasional pieces from contributors. In May of 1847, Van Rensselaer sent a file of *The Ram's Horn* to his friend Frederick Douglass with a request for an editorial contribution. In his lengthy response Douglass assented to the request, while praising Hodges and

---

[19]*Liberator*, 8 January 1847.

[20]*National Anti-Slavery Standard*, 7 January 1847.

[21]*The Ram's Horn*, June 1847, Reprinted in Herbert Aptheker, ed., *A Documentary History of the Negro People in the United States* (New York: The Citadel, 1951), 290-291.

Van Rensselaer's "gallant little sheet." He continued:

> I have given each number a hasty perusal, and have quite
> satisfied myself that you possess the energy of head and of
> heart to make your paper a powerful instrument in defend-
> ing, improving, and elevating our brethren in the (so
> called) free states, as well as hastening the downfall of the
> fierce and blood-thirsty *evangelical* [sic] tyrants in the
> slave States. Blow away on your "Ram's Horn"![22]

In August 1847, the *Liberator* acknowledged Douglass as
an assistant editor of *The Ram's Horn*. He suggested that the
editors change the paper's name to *The Fugitive American*.[23] However, he contributed little to *The Ram's Horn*
beyond the prestige associated with his name.[24] Douglass
himself later avowed that he had "never been a co-partner in
the 'Ram's Horn.'"[25] But after deciding to start a paper of his
own, he confided to a friend, J.D. Carr, that *The Ram's Horn*
would "probably be united with my paper."[26] Despite
Douglass' intentions, *The Ram's Horn* retained its name
and independent existence until its demise.

---

[22]Frederick Douglass to Thomas Van Rensselaer, 18 May 1847,
reprinted in *Liberator*, 4 June 1847.

[23]*Liberator*, 20 August 1847.

[24]Penn, 63. According to Penn, "Mr. Douglass, while he did little
writing for *The Ram's Horn*, was then so highly popular, that no paper was considered of much importance without the name of Douglass connected with it."

[25]*North Star*, 8 December 1848.

[26]Frederick Douglass to J.D. Carr, 1 November 1847. Reprinted in
The National Anti-Slavery Standard, 27 January 1848.

Another noteworthy contributor to *The Ram's Horn* was abolitionist John Brown. Hodges first became acquainted with Brown, who at the time was in the wool business in Springfield, Mass., through *The Ram's Horn*. Brown was one of many businessmen associated with the abolitionist movement who received complimentary copies of *The Ram's Horn*. According to Hodges, Brown visited the newspaper many times and also provided financial support. After receiving the complimentary copies, Brown sent a list of names and some money to the paper, along with the request that copies be mailed to people on the list for one year.[27] Impressed by articles that Hodges published on his experiences as a free black man in Virginia, Brown proposed a meeting with Hodges in the office of *The Ram's Horn*. According to Alexander Moore, a Hodges descendant with access to family papers, the two met in the office "as brothers, parted as friends; they related their past life, their futures were full of hope, their past histories had been different, their hopes were the same."[28]

Through this relationship, Hodges convinced Brown to publish his famous essay, "Sambo's Mistakes," in *The Ram's Horn* early in 1848. Brown believed that blacks were not doing all they could toward self-improvement. In "Sambo's Mistakes," he posed as a black man named Sambo who lampooned the weak and erroneous tactics of free blacks in the North and offered to his brethren the benefit of his experience. A portion of the lengthy article read:

Another error of my riper years has been, that when any meeting of colored people has been called in order to consider any important matter of general interest, I have been

---

[27]Gatewood, 78.

[28]Moore, Addendum, I.

so eager to display my spouting talents, and so tenacious of some trifling theory or other that I have adopted, that I have generally lost all sight of the business at hand, consumed the time disputing about things of no moment, and thereby defeated entirely many important measures calculated to promote the general welfare; but I am happy to say I can see in a minute where I missed it.

Another small error of my life (for I never committed great blunders) has been that I never would (for the sake of union in the furtherance of the most vital interests of our race) yield any minor point of difference. In this way I have always been to act with but a few, or more frequently alone, and could accomplish nothing worth living for; but I have one comfort, I can see in a minute where I missed it.[29]

Brown also shared Hodges' strong interest in blacks' quest to be self-sufficient through learning and practicing agricultural skills. Hodges used the columns of *The Ram's Horn* to encourage others to join him in taking advantage of Gerrit Smith's benevolent offer of free farmland. He argued that to own land was to escape "the doubtful employment and high rents of the city." There was also the guarantee that children would not become "victims of vice" as did so many who were forced to grow up in the city. Brown eagerly supported Hodges' endeavors and ultimately moved his family to the Adirondacks near the site where Hodges later settled.[30]

Hodges eventually decided to avail himself of Smith's offer, and on October 27, 1847, he received from Smith his

---

[29]F.B. Sanborn, ed., *The Life and Letters of John Brown* (Boston: Roberts Brothers, 1891), 129.

[30]*The Ram's Horn*, 5 November 1847.

deed to 40 acres of land in the Ninth Township of Franklin County near Loon Lake and Merrillsville in New York.[31] He then announced his plans to move there in the following spring. A "public entertainment" sponsored by the New York Emigration Association was held on April 20, 1848, to raise funds to assist those in Kings County, N.Y., who intended to settle on the Smith lands. Dissension between Hodges and Van Rensselaer—the specific nature of which is not clear—apparently made Hodges' decision to leave much easier. He sold his interest in *The Ram's Horn* to Van Rensselaer and in May 1848 led a group of black families to the Adirondacks to their new homes.[32] Hodges wrote:

> Soon after we started the "Ram's Horn" the question of moving out here on the Smith lands became one of importance, and I feared it, as it had always been my idea. I wrote several articles in the "Ram's Horn" a few months ago, the result of which, we, prisoners of the movement, find ourselves (through the mercy of God and the goodness of the honorable Garret [sic] Smith) to-day "under our own vine and fig trees," with none to molest or make us afraid.[33]

Hodges continued his involvement in politics, becoming a delegate to the national conventions of colored people, as well as the state constitutional convention in Virginia after the Civil War. He spoke often on suffrage, education, economic opportunities, and other issues of major concern to his

---

[31]Photocopy of the deed in the possession of Ms. Sandra Walker, Willis Hodges' great-granddaughter.

[32]Gatewood, xliii-xliv.

[33]Ibid., 80.

constituents.[34] However, he lost his political seat in Virginia to the local Republican Party, and returned to New York. Despite his declining health, he resumed his whitewashing business and continued to act as a minister in local churches. Shortly after returning home to Virginia, he died on September 24, 1890, at the age of 75. Few black newspapers took notice of his death. Those that did include brief obituaries referred to him as "an old time abolitionist," as a friend of John Brown, or as the founder of *The Ram's Horn*.[35]

Hodges had been "the soul of the 'Ram's Horn.'" Thus, it was no surprise that the newspaper he had founded suspended publication within months of his departure. Under Van Rensselaer, *The Ram's Horn* continued publication until July 1848 when he announced his intentions to move the paper to Toronto, Canada. However, there is no indication that the move was made, and the paper may have continued to appear irregularly until August of 1849. In October 1849, Van Rensselaer declared that *The Ram's Horn* was being "revived" and would be published in Philadelphia, but there is no evidence that it was revived.[36]

Despite high circulation figures and the support of influential blacks and whites throughout the North, *The Ram's Horn* suffered the same fate as its predecessors. It had pro-

------

[34]See, for example, *The Debates and Proceedings of the Constitutional Convention of the State of Virginia, 1867-1868* (Richmond: Office of the New Nation, 1868); and Howard H. Bell, ed., *Minutes of the Proceedings of the National Negro Conventions, 1830-1864* (New York: Arno Press, 1969).

[35]New York *Age*, 4 October 1890; and *Plaindealer* (Detroit), 8 October 1890.

[36]*North Star*, 14 July and 13 October 1848; 4 May and 26 October 1849.

vided news and a forum for a readership that had been denied the chance to be heard by one of the major mainstream paper in the area, the New York *Sun*, eventually establishing a circulation of close to 3,000. Its editors were staunch advocates of a variety of black causes, including antislavery, suffrage rights, financial independence, and education. All were causes Hodges felt it his duty as a free man of color to address and champion. Slavery was a major part of those issues, as were so many others. In his eyes, each concern was part of the struggle to return to blacks the rights earned by all Americans in the battle with England—"those sacred and God-given rights that their [whites] fathers and fathers' fathers have so unjustly, taken from us, to-wit: 'Life, liberty and the pursuit of happiness.'"[37]

Although its failure could not be attributed to the absence of initiative by the editors or a scarcity of causes to support, *The Ram's Horn* ceased to exist, like so many black-owned newspapers before it. Hodges' paper had served to replace all the papers of note that had failed a few years before while fighting for the rights of the oppressed man of color, and *The Ram's Horn* had helped to advance the development of the black press closer to its ultimate goal.

---

[37]Gatewood, 80.

4

THE *NORTH STAR*:
ABOLITIONIST OR ELEVATOR?

The November 5, 1847, issue of *The Ram's Horn* ushered in a new black-owned newspaper soon to become the voice of New York blacks. The advertisement read:

> PROSPECTUS for an anti-slavery paper, to be entitled NORTH STAR. Frederick Douglass proposes to publish in Rochester a weekly Anti-slavery paper, with the above title. The object of the NORTH STAR will be to attack Slavery in all its forms and aspects; Advocate Universal Emancipation; exalt the standard Public Morality; promote the Moral and Intellectual improvement of the COLORED PEOPLE; and hasten the day of FREEDOM to the Three Millions of our Enslaved Fellow Countrymen.[1]

The *North Star* was to become part of Frederick Douglass' plans for "renovating the public mind, and building up a public sentiment, which should send slavery to the grave, and restore 'liberty and the pursuit of happiness' to the

---

[1] *The Ram's Horn*, 5 November 1847.

people with whom I had suffered."[2] Noted for his eloquence and prowess in addressing the public, Douglass was an ex-slave and abolitionist who had also been associated with Willis Hodges' *The Ram's Horn*. The literary quality of his letters had been recognized by newspaper men such as the New York *Tribune's* Horace Greeley and the Albany *Evening Journal's* Thurlow Weed, noted journalists of the period. Greeley wrote that one of Douglass' letters to abolitionist William Lloyd Garrison had contained passages which "for genuine eloquence, would do honor to any writer of the English language." Weed judged Douglass as "among the most gifted and eloquent men of the age."[3]

Despite this talent for writing, Douglass was hesitant about establishing his own newspaper. Months earlier he had abandoned plans to establish his own newspaper at the advice of Garrison, who felt that:

> With such powers of oratory, and so few lecturers in the field where so many are needed, it seems to us as clear as the noon-day sun, that it would be no gain, but rather a loss, to the anti-slavery cause, to have him withdrawn to any considerable extent from the work of popular agitation, by assuming the cares, drudgery and perplexities of a publishing life.[4]

Garrison also pointed out the impracticality of attempting to combine the duties of editor and lecturer without causing a

---

[2]Frederick Douglass, *Life and Times of Frederick Douglass* (Hartford, Conn.: Park Publishing Co., 1882), 320.

[3]*Liberator*, 13 February 1846.

[4]*Liberator*, 23 July 1847.

certain amount of neglect in both areas.[5] Douglass defended his change of heart to his New England supporters in a letter to the editor of the Boston *Daily Whig*, citing the existence of three black-owned newspapers as "sufficient to accomplish the good which I sought."[6]

However, the discrimination Douglass faced in a lecture tour of the western United States convinced him that his decision to abandon the project of establishing a black-owned newspaper was an error in judgment. He believed that only someone who had suffered the indignities of racial discrimination could fully understand and express the plight of blacks. He wrote to an English friend on November 1, 1847, "I had not decided against the publication of a paper one month before I became satisfied that I had made a mistake, and each subsequent month's experience has confirmed me in the conviction."[7]

Douglass appealed to his friends in the United States and Great Britain for moral and financial support in his venture, although many reminded him of the failures of past newspapers established by blacks. However, he reasoned,

A tolerably well conducted press, by calling out the mental energies of the race itself; by making them acquainted with their own latent powers; by enkindling among them the hope that for them there is a future; by developing their moral power, by combining and reflecting their talents would prove a most powerful means of removing preju-

---

[5]Ibid.

[6]*Liberator*, 9 July 1847.

[7]Frederick Douglass to J.D. Carr, 1 November 1847. Reprinted in *National Anti-Slavery Standard*, 27 January 1848.

dice, and of awakening an interest in them.[8]

With $2,175 donated by friends in Great Britain, Douglass purchased a printing press and the necessary printing materials to begin operations at his new paper.[9] He selected Rochester, N.Y., as the site of operations so as not to interfere with the circulation of the *Liberator* and the *National Anti-Slavery Standard*.[10] The editors were Douglass and Martin R. Delany, former editor of the Pittsburgh *Mystery*. Delany's primary job was to travel throughout the country soliciting subscriptions, while Douglass was to remain in Rochester to write columns and to edit the paper. William C. Nell, a devoted Garrisonian and self-taught Negro, was listed as publisher. Douglass' children assisted in the printing and mailing operations, along with two white apprentices.[11]

Douglass modeled the page make-up and typography of his paper after such abolitionist papers as the *Liberator* and the *National Anti-Slavery Standard*. The *North Star* consisted of four pages of seven columns each. The first page was usually devoted to the full text of antislavery speeches in congressional meetings, state and national abolitionists' conventions, or antislavery meetings. The second page contained editorials by either Douglass or *North Star* correspondents such as James McCune Smith, a noted black

---

[8]Frederick Douglass, *My Bondage and My Freedom* (New York: Miller, Orton & Mulligan, 1885), 389-390.

[9]Ibid.

[10]Douglass, *Life*, 322.

[11]Philip S. Foner, ed., *The Life and Writings of Frederick Douglass* (New York: International Publishers, 1950), 84.

physician, or William G. Allen, a teacher at Central College in New York. The remaining two pages generally featured announcements, items clipped from other sources—such as poetry, literature reviews, and anecdotes—and advertisements.

The first issue of the *North Star* appeared on December 3, 1847. The masthead proclaimed, "Right is of no Sex—Truth is of no Color—God is the Father of Us All, And All We Are Brethren." The first issue included reports on the proceedings of the National Convention of Colored Americans held in Troy, N.Y.; black suffrage; a Henry Clay speech against the United States acquiring more land in which slavery would be introduced; and an open letter to Clay from Douglass opposing Clay's position on colonization. Clay supported the idea of black emigration. Douglass, like most of the abolitionists after 1830, believed that the promoters of colonization merely wished to secure slavery practices by ridding the country of free blacks.

In that first issue Douglass also included an editorial, "To Our Oppressed Countrymen," which addressed the aims of the editors. It read in part:

> While our paper shall be mainly Anti-Slavery, its columns shall be freely opened to the candid and decorous discussion of all measures and topics of a moral and human character, which may serve to enlighten, improve, and elevate mankind. Temperance, Peace, Capital Punishment, Education—all subjects claiming the attention of the public mind may be freely and fully discussed here.
>
> While advocating your rights, the North Star will strive to throw light on your duties: while it will not fail to make known your virtues, it will not shun to discover your faults. To be faithful to ourselves in all things.[12]

Douglass adamantly adhered to this pledge, contributing writings that became the mainstay of the paper. Aware of the limitations imposed by his lack of formal education, Douglass avidly read a variety of books, pamphlets, and tracts in the effort to increase his knowledge. The results were evident in his columns—in the high standards he set for himself and his contributors and in his penetrating analyses of his topics. That Douglass' *North Star* was strongly abolitionist is hardly surprising. Douglass declared himself to be a loyal follower of William Lloyd Garrison "and fully committed to his doctrine touching the pro-slavery character of the Constitution of the United States."[13] Garrison and his followers regarded the Constitution as an instrument of the slaveholders, designed to maintain and perpetuate the system of slavery. Douglass was as outspoken against slavery as his mentor Garrison, and his editorials were a strong feature of the *North Star*. One such editorial on antislavery and colonization appeared in the January 26, 1849, issue. It read:

> For two hundred and twenty-eight years has the colored man toiled over the soil of America, under a burning sun and a driver's lash—plowing, planting, reaping, that white men might roll in ease, their hands unhardened by labor, and their brows unmoistened by the waters of genial toil; and now that the moral sense of mankind is beginning to revolt at this system of foul treachery and cruel wrong, and is demanding its overthrow, the mean and cowardly oppressor is meditating plans to expel the colored

---

[12]*North Star*, 3 December 1847.

[13]Douglass, *Life*, 322.

man entirely from the country.[14]

Douglass' antislavery editorials were as powerful as his speeches. However, antislavery provided the basis for an eventual breach in the relationship between Douglass and Garrison. During the first four years of the paper's operation, Douglass espoused the Garrisonian position that the Constitution was a pro-slavery document which promoted the disenfranchisement of blacks. Garrison believed that non-slaveholding states were obligated to dissolve their union with the country's slaveholding states.[15] Douglass eventually concluded, after much reconsideration, that the Constitution demanded the abolition of slavery "as a condition of its own existence as the supreme law of the land."[16] Thereafter, he felt it was his duty to utilize political action, as well as moral power and literary activities, for emancipation rather than to continue to oppose the Constitution—severing his relationship with the Garrisonians and altering his stance in subsequent editorials and speeches.[17]

While the *North Star* served as a voice for the antislavery movement, it also became an organ of leadership for free blacks in the North. Douglass encouraged a peaceful coexistence between blacks and whites in everyday life. Separate activities, Douglass concluded, were conducive to ideas of black inferiority. In his series on black churches which excluded white participants, he even admonished his own race

---

[14]*North Star*, 26 January 1849.

[15]See, for example, *North Star*, 16 March 1849.

[16]Douglass, *Life*, 322.

[17]See, for example, *Liberator*, 16 May and 23 May 1851.

for attempting to keep the races segregated.[18] When his own daughter was denied the right to take classes in the same room with white young ladies at the Seward Seminary in Rochester, he wrote a detailed account of the incident of discrimination and Rosetta Douglass' subsequent enrollment in an equally "respectable" and "christian" school.[19]

Douglass' weekly reflected his concern about all problems resulting from clearly demarcated color lines. The paper also included reports of black achievements and articles which encouraged blacks to use their individual talents to succeed in day-to-day life. For example, the October 31, 1850, issue contained an article on "Mr. Hall," a black artisan who had surmounted the difficulties of racial prejudice to attain "a respectable position" and was now willing to employ two black teenagers as apprentices "to assist others of his oppressed race to follow his noble example."[20]

Like his black predecessors who established their own newspapers, Douglass addressed a variety of topics necessary to the improvement and elevation of blacks—self-determination, education, temperance, good moral principles. He believed that self-motivation was as important to the advancement of blacks as was racial unity. In an editorial, "What are the Colored People Doing for Themselves," Douglass pointed out:

The fact that we are limited and circumscribed, ought rather to incite us to a more vigorous and persevering use of the elevating menus [sic] within our reach, than to dis-

---

[18]*North Star*, 25 February 1848 - 10 March 1848.

[19]*North Star*, 30 March 1849.

[20]*North Star*, 31 October 1850.

hearten us. The means of education, though not so free and open to us as to white persons, are nevertheless at our command to such an extent as to make education possible....[21]

The importance of education appeared frequently in the columns of the *North Star*. Douglass saw education and knowledge as the only avenue to overcome prejudice and social inequality. According to Douglass, "a rigid economy in the expenditure of money, and the elevation of a high standard of morality," along with the acquisition of knowledge, were the means to this end.[22]

Moral issues such as temperance, idleness, and good character were also components in Douglass' pattern for advancement. He wrote:

The elevation of a high standard of morality is an indispensable requisite for our advancement. We are living in a land, where, on the side of the oppressor there is power, and every dereliction on our part is trumpeted forth as a giant offence; it behoves [sic] us, therefore, to be careful in our morals, that at least, we may be conscious of being in the right.[23]

Douglass also became an advocate for women's rights, pleading the cause for education for females. In an editorial against statements made in the *U.S. Gazette* of Philadel-

---

[21]*North Star*, 14 July 1848.

[22]*North Star*, 20 April 1849. See also, for example, *North Star*, 17 March 1848; 4 February 1848; and 21 April 1848.

[23]*North Star*, 4 May 1849.

phia, he declared that "what is a home, where there is no intellect—no cultivation—no refinement—no knowledge,
save that which partakes of menial duties?"[24]

Public reaction to the first few months of the *North Star*
was mixed. There were those who regarded the paper as "a
blemish and a misfortune" for the city of Rochester. The
New York *Herald* advised the people to throw Douglass'
printing press into Lake Ontario and to banish the editor to
Canada.[25] The Albany *Sunday Dispatch* warned citizens
that the paper was a "serious detriment" to the community
and suggested that they "buy him [Douglass] off."[26] Fortu-
nately for Douglass and the *North Star*, local hostility was
minimal and of short duration. There were also those individuals and groups who applauded the newspaper. The Garrisonians, who had originally been opposed to Douglass'
plans for the paper, reluctantly expressed limited support.[27]
The Rochester *Daily Advertiser* noted the neatness of the
paper's appearance, the "high order of talent" evident in the
lead article, and the editor as "a man of much more than
[the] ordinary share of intellect."[28]

The *North Star* continued to gain support over the years.
It eventually established an average circulation of 3,000 sub-
scribers, but the early years of operation were difficult.
North Star readers included blacks and whites in the North

---

[24]*North Star*, 17 March 1848.

[25]Douglass, *Life*, 326.

[26]*North Star*, 21 January 1848.

[27]See, for example, *National Anti-Slavery Standard*, 27 January
1848; and *Liberator*, 28 January 1848.

[28]Rochester *Daily Advertiser*, 18 December 1847.

and South, as well as in Europe.[29] However, as of May 1848 the *North Star* had five white subscribers for every black subscriber.[30] Douglass was angered by this apparent apathy and lack of support. In one of his scathing editorials he wrote,

> Tell them [blacks] that a well conducted press in the hands of colored men is essential to the progress and elevation of the colored man, and they will regard you as one merely seeking a living at public expense, "to get along without work."[31]

However, he seems to have failed to consider the financial straits of free blacks of the period. Delany encountered this obstacle during his travels to garner subscriptions. Circulation problems were undoubtedly part of the reason for the dissolution of his partnership with Douglass. With a mailing list of scarcely seven hundred at the beginning of 1848, Douglass complained to Delany, who was on a subscription tour, "Subscribers come in slowly, and I am doing all I can by lectures and letters to keep our heads above water."[32] However, Delany was continually unable to raise funds for the paper. By the July 6, 1848, issue, the *North Star* was under the sole editorship of Douglass, and it contained a paragraph informing the public that all mail for Delany was to be dis-

---

[29]See, for example, "Correspondence," *North Star*, 26 April 1850.

[30]Benjamin Quarles, *Frederick Douglass* (Washington, D.C.: The Associated Publishers, Inc., 1948), 89.

[31]*North Star*, 27 April 1849.

[32]Frederick Douglass to Martin R. Delany, 12 January 1848. Reprinted in Foner, 85.

patched to his new address in Pittsburgh. Delany went on to study medicine and to establish an important career in that field.

Despite rising financial difficulties and Delany's departure, Douglass continued to publish the paper, and he praised the accomplishments of the first year of operation. To his readers he reaffirmed his idea that a large weekly newspaper under the editorial management of blacks would be an overwhelming instrument to help abolish slavery, to dispel claims of black inferiority, and to remove the shadow of prejudice.[33] By the second year, he was convinced that the *North Star* was fulfilling its obligations to slaves and free blacks. He noted that the paper "ought, must, and (as far as our *fiat* can go) shall be sustained." He implored his supporters to "[l]et all doubts be removed, and let readers and friends unite to help those who are at least *deserving* it—in that they display a willingness to help themselves."[34]

Douglass' efforts to sustain the paper were possible with the help of donations, lecture fees, and funds raised by his British friend Julia Griffiths. As with the previous black-owned newspapers, financial burdens began to take their toll on Douglass and the *North Star*. After the first year, Douglass had mortgaged his home and the paper itself was $200 in debt. Griffiths took charge of the finances for the paper in the summer of 1848 and separated Douglass' personal finances from those of the paper. She devised numerous projects to raise funds for the paper, including sponsoring fairs and mailing personal appeals for financial aid to potential backers. Griffiths also built a strong movement among the woman abolitionists in Rochester, garnering their support

---

[33]*North Star*, 22 December 1848.

[34]*North Star*, 14 December 1849.

in fund-raising efforts.[35] The financial strain began to ease, and Douglass reported to philanthropist Gerrit Smith that the "'North Star' sustains itself and partly my large family. It has just reached a living point. Hitherto the struggle of its life has been to live. Now it more than lives."[36]

Douglass' financial situation was further improved by an agreement with Smith to merge with the *Liberty Party Paper*, a weekly edited and published by John Thomas of Syracuse. Douglass' conversion to political abolitionism, the use of the words of the Constitution as an instrument for antislavery, and the prestige associated with his name made Douglass a beneficial addition to the staff of the failing Liberty party organ. Smith, the financial backer for the *Liberty Party Paper*, promised to assume the debts of the *North Star* and to make monthly donations to support the new paper. In exchange, Douglass was to act as editor of the new publication with Thomas as the assistant editor and Julia Griffiths as the business manager.[37] The name of the paper was changed to *Frederick Douglass' Paper* "in order to distinguish it from the many papers with 'Stars' in their titles."[38] Douglass probably also believed that the use of his name might help to increase circulation figures. The new motto, proposed by Smith, was "All Rights For All."

Douglass' paper was basically a continuation of the *North Star* with occasional news of Liberty party activities.

---

[35]Foner, 87-88.

[36]Frederick Douglass to Gerrit Smith, 1 May 1851, Gerrit Smith Papers, Syracuse University, Syracuse, N.Y.

[37]Foner, 89.

[38]Douglass, *Life*, 325.

A noticeable change, however, was the absence of the familiar "F.D." at the end of Douglass' articles. According to Douglass, the initials had been proof to doubters that a fugitive slave with no formal education could make effective use of the English language. After three years, this fact had clearly been established, and he was assuming "in full the right and dignity of an *Editor*—a Mr. Editor if you please."[39]

Douglass maintained his conviction that a black leader should speak out against race-oriented problems facing blacks. In his role as editor of the *North Star*, he had made a special effort to increase his contact with blacks and their daily problems. He continued this practice with *Frederick Douglass' Paper*. He regularly included accounts of his personal struggles against segregation. However, his most severe editorials were directed toward blacks who passively accepted discrimination. He attacked Elizabeth Greenfield, known as "the Black Swan," for her practice of singing at concerts that blacks were excluded from attending. In Douglass' eyes, she had betrayed the cause of her people. "She should be called no longer the *Black Swan*," he wrote, "but the White Raven."[40]

For two years, *Frederick Douglass' Paper* was able to meet its expenses with the help of Gerrit Smith's monthly donations. However, delinquent subscription fees and Smith's decreased donations after 1852 added to Douglass' worries. Griffiths launched a campaign to raise $1,000 in 10-dollar donations to help toward sustaining the paper. By January of 1854 she had collected only $420.[41] William Johnson, one of

---

[39]*Frederick Douglass' Paper*, 26 June 1851.

[40]*Frederick Douglass' Paper*, 8 April 1855.

[41]Foner, 89.

the black contributors to the fund, offered this appeal to the blacks of the city:

> ...If there is any one thing more than another, that we need in a public way as a fixture, it is that of a newspaper, conducted and published by a colored man, through which our views and sentiments may be known as a people; and since God has raised up as a man in the person of Frederick Douglass, who has demonstrated to the world that he has the ability to vindicate the rights of man, with equal force, either on platform as an orator, or as an editor of a newspaper, it becomes the duty of every colored man and woman to sustain Frederick Douglass and his paper.[42]

Supporters were slow to step forward. Financial difficulties continued to multiply, and by 1856 the paper was $1,500 in debt.[43] Griffiths advised Douglass to appeal to his British friends for help. In 1858 he issued *Douglass' Monthly*, a journal smaller in size than *Frederick Douglass' Paper* and offered only in the British Isles. The following year he was forced to reduce the size of *Frederick Douglass' Paper*, but weekly expenses continued to rise. By 1860 cash receipts were nearly zero, due to delinquent subscribers and increased publication costs. On July 2, 1860, Douglass wrote Smith of his decision to end the paper:

> You may well believe that after nearly thirteen years of effort to put the paper on a permanent basis and make it an established anti-slavery instrumentality, that I am now very sorry to give up the struggle. There is no escape and I

---

[42]*Frederick Douglass' Paper*, 9 January 1854.

[43]Quarles, 91.

submit. I shall hereafter only publish my monthly paper.[44]

Douglass published his monthly for three years before he ceased operations. For the next decade, he remained active on the lecture circuit and in politics. He returned to journalism in 1870 as corresponding editor for a new Washington weekly, the *New Era*. It failed in 1875 after costing Douglass $10,000 in operating expenses. He then returned to his political activities and continued until his death in 1895 at the age of 78.[45]

The *North Star* and *Frederick Douglass' Paper* had suffered the fate common among Douglass' predecessors, but he had managed to succeed where they had failed. It was no small accomplishment to conduct a black-owned, advocacy-oriented newspaper for almost 13 years during the pre-Civil War era. As the importance of the slavery issue intensified, Douglass increased his emphasis on its evils in the columns of his newspaper. He was also concerned with the difficulties of black life. Therefore, he dealt with those problems emanating from slavery and offered insight into black advancement. Thus, Douglass fulfilled his duties as newspaper editor and black leader: to provide information, to offer guidance, and to encourage others to continue in their efforts toward social improvement.

---

[44]Douglass to Gerrit Smith, 2 July 1860, Gerrit Smith Papers, Syracuse University, Syracuse, N.Y.

[45]Wolseley, 23.

5

A FREE VOICE

Of the various factors contributing to the development of the black press, the opportunity for free expression occurred more frequently than any others—whether in the circumstances surrounding the newspapers' creation or the editors' originally stated goals. In each instance, the editors had either been denied access to the white press or had determined that black interests were not being served in the existing mainstream newspapers. Their commitment to observing the informational and advocacy-oriented needs of blacks was portrayed in the papers' original statements of purpose and subsequent editorials.

Hodges' *The Ram's Horn* was a result of both limited access and the need for a newspaper which served as a black spokesman. He had already noted that the failure of previous black-owned newspapers in New York had left black residents without a public voice, and his personal confrontation with the *Sun* editor convinced him that a black publication would be the only solution.

Likewise, the New York *Enquirer* refused to print letters by Samuel Cornish and John Russwurm in response to the paper's attacks on New York City's black residents. *Freedom's Journal's* statement of purpose subsequently avowed that the editors would plead the causes of the black people and disprove previous misrepresentations of the race.

Phillip A. Bell, founder of the *Colored American*, noted the lack of a black spokesman after the termination of *Freedom's Journal*, followed by the rapid demise of its New York successors, and the desire for a newspaper devoted to the specific interests of blacks. He declared that his paper would be an "advocate" for the black community—hence, the paper's original name of the *Weekly Advocate*. According to the *Advocate's* statement of purpose, the paper was to be a black-owned and black-managed publication devoted particularly to the interests of the city's black population.

Despite his association with abolitionists and their newspapers, Frederick Douglass believed that only someone who had personally experienced racial discrimination could fully understand the problems and concerns of the black population in the United States. Douglass proclaimed that the columns of the *North Star* would become a forum for the discussion of topics ranging from antislavery to moral and human character.

The creators of all four newspapers seemed to determine that the black community required a public spokesman to champion their causes and to advise them on topics necessary for their social improvement. This was undoubtedly the case for the majority of the approximately 40 black-owned newspapers started prior to the Civil War. As blacks themselves, these editors and publishers felt that they could empathize with the plight of black Americans and were better qualified to judge what topics would best serve black interests. The issues addressed most often and which occupied the majority of news space can be categorized into the following groups: Slavery, Political Activism/Civil Rights, Personal Improvement, Moral Elevation, and Racial Equality.

Slavery

Slavery, the issue cited most often by early historians as

the primary reason behind the creation of the minority press, did not receive as much attention as early historians had determined. However, slavery was an inescapable reality in the lives of black Americans and could not be overlooked by those men who designated themselves as spokesmen for the race. Items pertaining to slavery included such topics as colonization, antislavery speeches and convention minutes, and antislavery editorials.

Slavery appeared to be less of an issue for the two earlier newspapers in the study, *Freedom's Journal* and the *Colored American*. The abomination of slavery had not reached the magnitude of importance it would attain by the 1850s, and the antislavery movement was just beginning. There was also little chance that the newspapers would ever reach the slave population in the South, and the contents were directed more toward the free blacks and former slaves residing in the North. Attacks on slavery were cautious and subtle, with the exception of occasional sarcastic pieces aimed at slavery and slaveowners. However, *Freedom's Journal* editors Samuel Cornish and John Russwurm were particularly outspoken on the colonization issue, which later contributed to Cornish's departure from the paper. Cornish continued to oppose colonization in his second paper, the *Colored American*, denouncing it as a plot to deny blacks the same rights conferred on their white counterparts. The editors of the *Colored American* also included warnings about kidnappers and the illegal arrests of free blacks as fugitive slaves.

By the 1850s, the importance of slavery had intensified due to the division between slaveholders and non-slaveholders which had taken on nationwide proportions and the threats of Southern states to secede from the Union. Willis Hodges of *The Ram's Horn* was more outspoken about his opposition to slavery than Cornish and Russwurm, while Frederick Douglass patterned his *North Star* after noted abolitionist papers in the state. Editorials by Hodges and his friend, abolitionist John Brown, exhorted blacks to resist slavery and to work toward improving themselves. Similarly, Douglass covered his front pages with the complete text of antislavery speeches in public and at congressional meetings, antislavery meetings, and the minutes of local and national colored conventions. The second page of the newspaper was usually devoted to editorials, many antislavery-oriented.

In its role of informing the readers, the black press presented slavery as a predominant issue in its newspaper pages only as its effects began to make a significant impact on the country and its ramifications reached nationwide proportions. There were many other equally important topics which were instrumental in motivating the papers' editors, publishers, and supporters.

Political Activism/Civil Rights

The encouragement of black involvement in politics was also a predominant theme for the newspapers. Editors participated in a variety of political causes and urged their readers to do likewise. By so doing, blacks could assume a larger role in the decisions that directed their lives. This interest in politics took the form of such topics as black suffrage, voting requirements, women's rights, and the introduction of slave states into the Union. Black suffrage rights and discriminatory voting requirements were indirectly responsible for Hodges' founding of *The Ram's Horn*. The paper's only extant issue included an article on blacks' responsibility to exercise their voting rights and to oppose the clause in the New York state constitution which required blacks to own $250 in real estate before they could vote.[1] In *Freedom's Journal* Cornish, likewise, stressed the importance of exercising voting rights, and he chastised those

---

[1] *The Ram's Horn*, 5 November 1847.

blacks who qualified but failed to participate in New York elections. Like Hodges, he also protested the qualification tests and financial restrictions which limited black participation.

Cornish conducted an equally vehement campaign against these restrictions in the *Colored American*, urging his readers to pursue the franchise issue further. He also advocated forming a new party when existing political parties proved unresponsive to the needs of black Americans.[2] Douglass supported this type of political involvement and extended advocacy of these civil rights to include women.

Unresponsiveness by white political and community leaders compelled black editors to turn to their own newspapers to plead the black cause. To these men, direct involvement in politics was the first step for blacks to take in order to gain control of their own lives and to help determine their own future existence.

Personal Improvement

Early black editors seemed to agree that a key component to improving the condition of blacks in the United States was personal improvement. From the outset of *Freedom's Journal*, Samuel Cornish declared that poverty, unemployment, and the lack of education and money-management skills were obstacles to be surmounted in the plan to establish a place for blacks in society.[3]

Topics pertaining to cultural and economic advancement included education (basic reading and writing as well as labor training), diligence in establishing good work

---

[2]See, for example, *Colored American*, 6 May 1837; 3 September 1837; and 10 October 1840.

[3]*Freedom's Journal*, 16 March 1827.

habits, self-determination, management of financial resources, and unity within the black community. Advice on
these subjects appeared in the forms of parables, personal experiences, and sometimes poetry. Editors of all four papers—
Cornish in particular—declared that education was the basis
for blacks' social development. Cornish called it "an object
of the highest importance to the welfare of society,"[4] while
Douglass considered education to be a solution for overcom-
ing prejudice and social inequality.[5] Cornish also urged
blacks to cultivate good habits of industry and to teach these
habits to their children.

Hodges was also a forceful advocate of industriousness,
particularly when achieved in an agricultural life.
Through agriculture and country living, he reasoned,
blacks could develop a sense of self-reliance, since owning
land was a means of ensuring employment and self-determination about opportunities for advancement. Cornish was
convinced that elevation was to be achieved through individual efforts and character. To his *Freedom's Journal*
readers, he offered advice on endeavoring to learn a trade
and encouraged them to be frugal in their spending habits
while investing the surplus income.

Despite the emphasis on individual advancement, Cornish never neglected the opportunity to stress the need for
racial unity—whether for the task of educating the black
population or instilling a set of moral principles in the
minds of children. He blamed the lack of racial unity for the
existence of slavery. Douglass also encouraged racial unity
not only in the community, but in support of his newspaper as

---

[4]Ibid.

[5]See, for example, *North Star*, 17 March 1848; 4 February 1848; and
21 April 1848.

---

well.

The idea of an industrious black race was prevalent among the editors of the four newspapers. Each one encouraged blacks to acquire knowledge, to learn a labor skill, and to direct the profits from employment toward a more stable lifestyle for future generations.

Moral Elevation

Editors treated the issue of moral elevation as significant for both adults and children. Advice for improving moral character ranged from warning blacks about practicing certain "vices" to encouraging parents to teach their children good moral principles. Moral themes included temperance, gambling, idleness, and charity. The newspapers featured profiles of blacks of high social standing and of good moral character to serve as role models for the community.

Both Douglass and Hodges devoted editorials to the destructive consequences of alcohol abuse. Cornish warned against the evils of gambling, particularly lotteries. Charles Bennett Ray, Cornish's successor at the *Colored American*, developed a regular column for the moral instruction of children as a way of directing them toward becoming useful and productive members of society. Douglass also considered a high standard of morality as imperative in the struggle to attain equal social standing.

This emphasis on moral behavior might also have been the result of the religious background of the editors and publishers. Some were ministers, while others were active participants in a variety of church-sponsored events.

Racial Equality

Racial equality, like slavery, received an increasing amount of coverage as the issue began to attract nationwide attention. Editors of the earliest papers concentrated on promoting the rights of blacks in such areas as education and employment. As long as facilities and employment opportunities were available to blacks, the editors displayed little concern over segregation.

However, Douglass deplored segregation of any kind and warned his readers that segregation helped to sustain the idea that blacks were inferior to whites. He directed some of his more passionate editorials toward his own race for such actions as holding church services that excluded whites or performing in public facilities which precluded black attendance.

Similarly, Hodges voiced outrage at the New York *Sun* editor who declared that the paper would represent only "white men, not black men." His paper, *The Ram's Horn*, was consequently dedicated to presenting news of interest to all people, regardless of race.

Implications

Despite many earlier historical implications to the contrary, slavery was only one of many concerns that necessitated the creation of an early black newspaper and helped to determine its contents. A plethora of recurring issues lends credence to the idea that no *one* concern provided the motivation for establishing the black press.

The one underlying thread of consistency among these major concerns was the obligation to improve the lifestyle of black Americans—whether in protesting injustices to the black population, attempting to correct those oversights, or to improve their financial situation and moral character. The right of blacks to be allowed to speak for themselves was treated as no less significant than their right to live as free Americans. Their need to improve their moral character was emphasized as much as the importance of economic improvement.

Prior to the Civil War, the black race was fragmented

due to such circumstances as education, bondage, employment, and social standing. Therefore, black individuals
maintained a variety of interests and outlooks. No newspaper dedicated to representing these individuals could be ex-
pected to favor only one of these concerns. The contents of the
early black newspapers and their mainstream and abolitionist counterparts, as well as the personal diaries and letters of the editors and publishers, reveal the complexity of the
reasoning which led to the development of the black press as
a forum of free expression.

Appendix A

HISTORIOGRAPHICAL ESSAY

Over the years, historians have given little attention to the development of the black press. Only brief references, seldom longer than one or two sentences, were made in most standard journalism history books. The central idea of much of the literature dealing to any degree with the early black press focused on slavery as the reason for its creation.

However, the research of later historians has revealed that other factors besides slavery might have been involved. Some of these factors may have had an impact on the philosophies of the black editors and publishers, as well as on the newspapers' content.

For example, Irving Garland Penn concluded that *Freedom's Journal*, the country's first black newspaper, was created to increase sentiment and interest in the plight of the Southern slaves.[1] But an examination of the *Journal's* objectives outlined in the first issue revealed only this reference to slavery:

And while these important subjects shall occupy the columns of FREEDOM's JOURNAL, we would not be unmindful of our brethren who are still in the iron fetters of

---

[1]Irving Garland Penn, *The Afro-American Press and Its Editors* (Springfield, Mass.: Wiley and Co., 1891).

bondage. They are our kindred by all the times of nature; and though but little can be effected by us, still let our sympathies be poured forth, and our prayers in their behalf, ascend to Him who is able to succour them.[2]

Based on the amount of space devoted to slavery in the *Journal's* list of objectives, this statement by editors Cornish and Russwurm could not be considered the issue of major concern for the newspaper. According to Carter G. Woodson, *Freedom's Journal* was created when the social atmosphere throughout the country was more favorable to literacy and education among blacks than at any time prior to the Civil War.[3]

Based on this premise, Henry La Brie, III, and Bella Gross offered what may be more, or at least equally, plausible reasons than those of Penn. La Brie theorized that Cornish and Russwurm realized it was finally the appropriate time for black Americans to voice their own opinions and establish a separate and distinct identity from the "white world" in which they lived.[4] Gross concluded that *Freedom's Journal* was the champion of the free blacks and was founded "to defend their citizenship rights, express their hopes and wishes."[5]

The founding of the black press may be better explained

---

[2]"To Our Patrons," *Freedom's Journal*, 16 March 1827, p. 1.

[3]Carter G. Woodson, *The Education of the Negro Prior to 1861* (New York:1915), 228.

[4]Henry La Brie, III, "Black Newspapers: The Roots are 150 Years Deep," *Journalism History* 4 (Winter 1977-78): 111-113.

[5]Bella Gross, "'Freedom's Journal' and the 'Rights of All,'" *Journal of Negro History* 17 (July 1932): 262.

by an alternative interpretation far more comprehensive than the topic of slavery provides.

Despite the abundance of available literature on journalism history, few studies have been done on the early black press. Like Mott, Tebbel, and Hudson in their general survey histories of American journalism, many historians limited their observations on the black press to a few sentences or paragraphs.[6]

Information resulting from the research conducted by those historians who attempted to study this period has often been inaccurate and contradictory. These discrepancies, coupled with the lack of accessibility to copies of the newspapers, have also made a thorough examination of this period difficult.

However, there were exceptions. Penn's *The Afro-American Press and Its Editors* documented not only the early black newspapers existing in America at the time, but included information on their editors, reporters, correspondents, and contributors. Penn concluded, as did many others, that any newspapers established in 1827 and the succeeding forty years were created to support the abolition of slavery.[7]

Penn, who was a newspaper correspondent, published his registry of black newspapers in the latter part of the century. While an important source of information, Penn's book often contained inaccurate information or overlooked some

---

[6]See, for example, Frank Luther Mott, *American Journalism* (New York: Macmillan, 1941); John Tebbel, *The Media in America* (New York: Thomas Y. Crowell, 1974); and Frederic Hudson, *Journalism in the United States, from 1690 to 1872* (New York: Harper and Row, 1873).

[7]Penn, *The Afro-American Press and Its Editors*.

significant points during the course of his research. However, his work has served as a starting point for many later historians.

Frederick Detwiler briefly offered a similar rationale to Penn's in *The Negro Press in the United States.* According to Detwiler, Cornish of *Freedom's Journal* set out to demonstrate that all evils that then existed were the direct result of slavery. Detwiler hypothesized that Cornish sought to prove that the blacks "were not any worse, but better, than the lower-class whites, since many of them had education, refinement, and wealth."[8]

Detwiler chronicles the development of the black press from slavery days to World War I. His information seems to have been drawn primarily from secondary sources, including Penn's book. His reasoning for the origin of the black press, cited in the chapter "The Negro Press in Slavery Days," appears to be a reiteration of past positions.

James Tinney and Justine Rector also offered an interpretation that considered slavery as the all-encompassing reason behind the start of the black press. They decided:

It was the peculiar institution of slavery, together with its attendant and subsequent manifestations, that caused Black [sic] men and women to register protest in printed form.[9]

They viewed the black press from a political standpoint and

---

[8]Frederick Detwiler, *The Negro Press in the United States* (Chicago: University of Chicago Press, 1922), 35.

[9]James S. Tinney and Justine J. Rector, eds., *Issues and Trends in Afro-American Journalism* (Lanham, Md.: University Press of America, 1980), 1.

determined that, "created in opposition to the political forces which threatened and destroyed Black men, the Black Press became in its own sense an early Black [sic] political institution concerned with the distribution of power"[10] and progress.

The book edited by Tinney and Rector is a collection of essays and articles written primarily in the 1970s, which deal with the role of blacks in politics through the use of the mass media. It falls short of a critical examination of the minority press because all the essays tend to judge the early black press by the standards and criteria of the 20th century press. From the viewpoint of the writers and editors, the black press over the last 160 years has been a militant presence in society. This militancy was, thus, a direct result of slavery.

However, to some of the historians of later years, slavery as the primary reason for the creation of the minority press was insufficient. They began to look for other less obvious reasons.

According to historian Gunnar Myrdal, the development of the black press followed two trends: the increase in strength of black protests against social injustice and the rise in the black literacy rate. Myrdal reasoned that this early period of militancy set the stage for later protests for civil liberties. With the larger number of blacks who could read, black editors and publishers finally had an audience that deserved to be represented.[11]

Armistead Pride viewed these black editors and publish-

---

[10]Ibid.

[11]Gunnar Myrdal, *An American Dilemma: The Negro Problem and Modern Democracy* (New York: Harper and Brothers Publishers, 1944).

ers as "black citizens interested in promoting the welfare of the free black population through the medium of a newspaper or magazine."[12] Similarly, Martin Dann pointed out two concerns prevalent in the black press: a response to white racism and an assertion of self-determination. Dann determined that black newspapers printed prior to the Civil War were not aimed at the slave population of the South. They were written to attract the upwardly mobile free blacks and ex-slaves residing predominantly in the North. The editors directed their columns

> ...primarily to the conditions at home, to kidnappers in New York, to various methods of self-help and self-improvement, to self-defense, to the colonization controversy rather than to conditions in the South upon which they felt they could have little direct influence.[13]

In an earlier interpretation, Gross presented an idea similar to that of Dann. Gross cited the goal of black newspapers, particularly *Freedom's Journal*, as the "universal-elevation of man, the secret of which lay in the arts and sciences to be cultivated by men working in harmony for the general good."[14] Gross continued, "Only a strange necessity, the editor [of the *Journal*] declared, forced them to stress 'race'; the cosmic outlook, the universal good, however, was

---

[12]Armistead Pride, "'Rights of All': Second Step in the Development of Black Journalism," *Journalism History* 4 (Winter 1977-78): 129.

[13]Martin E. Dann, ed. *The Black Press, 1827-1890: The Quest for National Unity* (New York: G.P. Putnam's Sons, 1971), 16.

[14]Gross, 246.

never sacrificed on the altar of race."[15]

However, Dann further stated that the black press offered blacks a chance to express their opinions freely. Prior to 1827, access to the white-owned newspapers was repeatedly denied.[16] Lionel C. Barrow, Jr., also pointed out that *Freedom's Journal* provided a forum for blacks to respond to the attacks, as well as to read articles on black accomplishments, marriages, births, and deaths.[17]

Dann's book is probably one of the more comprehensive studies made of the minority press. The book is an anthology of articles appearing in the early black newspapers. These are categorized based on the newspapers' portrayal of the black perspective on topics such as politics, labor, and American history.

Roland Wolseley expressed a viewpoint similar to those of Dann and Barrow in his book, *The Black Press, U.S.A.*, Wolseley viewed the founding of *Freedom's Journal* "as a means of answering attacks on blacks by another newspaper of that city, the white New York *Enquirer*."[18]

Wolseley's book is a comparison of the early black press and its 20th-century counterpart. It also examines the relationship between the press and the social movements involving blacks. Due to the enormity of his task, Wolseley allocates very little space to the origin of the black press. Chapter

---

[15]Ibid.

[16]Dann, 16.

[17]Lionel C. Barrow, Jr., "Our Own Cause: 'Freedom's Journal' and the Beginnings of the Black Press," *Journalism History* 4 (Winter 1977-78): 118-122.

[18]Roland Wolseley, *The Black Press, U.S.A.* (Ames: Iowa State University Press, 1971), 17-18.

Two, "The Beginnings," is only a brief summary of the appearance of black publications prior to the turn of the century. However, Wolseley does make the statement that the newspapers were probably aimed at a readership that would be of assistance to the free black man, unlike the columns of the white-owned *Enquirer.*

Likewise, Lauren Kessler considered a series of such printed attacks as a catalyst for the creation of several black newspapers. According to Kessler, the mainstream press remained closed and unresponsive to black issues and presented a closed "marketplace of ideas."

These publications, founded in response to the denial of access by the mainstream press, developed into independent forums providing information and inspiration. Kessler cited three aims of *Freedom's Journal*: reporting black accomplishments, encouraging strength of character, and seeking the abolition of slavery.[19]

Lee Finkle added another item to the list: opposition to the American Colonization Society. In the introduction to *Forum for Protest*, Finkle also concluded that Cornish and Russwurm founded *Freedom's Journal* to fight the attacks of white racism. He also attributed to the editors the purpose of opposing the organized colonization of free blacks in Africa. Finkle regarded Cornish as being "extremely hostile to the Colonization Society, and from the beginning he saw it as his duty to attack and expose the society in every issue of his paper."[20]

In his introduction to *The Black Press in the South, 1865-*

---

[19]Lauren Kessler, *The Dissident Press: Alternative Journalism in American History* (Beverly Hills: Sage Publications, 1984).

[20]Lee Finkle, *Forum for Protest* (Cranbury, N.J.: Associated University Presses, 1975), 18.

1979, Henry Lewis Suggs also mentioned the significance of the emigration-colonization controversy and the tendency of the journalists of the early black press to attempt to speak for the entire race.[21]

As Kenneth Nordin concluded, for black newspapers such as *Freedom's Journal* the concept of abolition was too narrow. While social injustice and the end of slavery were major concerns, there were broader journalistic objectives, including counteracting anti-black prejudice among whites, developing a sense of black fraternity, and emphasizing the potential for intellectual and cultural achievement.[22]

According to Gross, *Freedom's Journal*, the first black newspaper created in the United States, marked the beginning of a national movement among blacks and formed the basis of a "Negro Renaissance." Gross noted:

Although a "race-paper," created for the express purpose of fighting slavery and of voicing the thoughts and hopes of the free people of color, the outlook of the *Journal*, its interests, and appeal were universal. In its desire to get at the roots of things, it went to the vast store of universal learning, to history, philosophy, and science; it solicited the opinions of all kinds of people, and of friends as well as enemies. Race issues were but parts of the universal problems which man had to solve, and which he could solve

---

[21]Henry Lewis Suggs, ed., *The Black Press in the South, 1865-1979* (Westport, Conn.: Greenwood Press, 1983).

[22]Kenneth Nordin, "In Search of Black Unity: An Interpretation of the Content and Function of "Freedom's Journal,'" *Journalism History* 4 (Winter 1977-78): 123-128.

only by cooperating.[23]

Such statements lend credence to the idea that the founding of the black press was far more complex than the somewhat limited explanation of slavery, and the black press played a significant role in the development of American society. While slavery was indeed a major concern, there were other issues besides slavery to consider during that time period prior to the Civil War.

---

[23]Gross, 245-246.

Appendix B

WORKS CITED

Primary Sources

Anglo-American. 1859.

Bell, Howard H., ed. "Proceedings of the National Convention of Colored People and their Friends, October 6-9, 1847." *Minutes of the Proceedings of the National Negro Convention, 1830-1864.* New York: Arno Press, 1969.

Colored American. 1837-1841.

Debates and Proceedings of the Constitutional Convention of the State of Virginia, 1867-1868. Richmond: Office of the New Nation, 1868.

Delany, Martin Robison. *The Condition, Elevation, Emigration, and Destiny of the Colored People of the United States.* Philadelphia: By the author, 1852.

Douglass, Frederick. *My Bondage and My Freedom.* New York: Miller, Orton & Mulligan, 1885.

_____. *Life and Times of Frederick Douglass.* Hartford, Conn.: Park Publishing Co., 1882.

Frederick Douglass' Paper. 1851-1855.

Freedom's Journal. 1827-1829.

Garrison, William Lloyd, correspondence in the Villard Papers, Harvard College Library, Cambridge.

Gerrit Smith Papers, Syracuse University, Syracuse, N.Y.

Liberator. 1831-1851.

Minutes of the Pennsylvania Society for Promoting the Abolition of Slavery (1827-1847). Philadelphia: Historical Society of Pennsylvania, n.d.

Moore, Alexander. *Nelson-Hodges Papers, 1773-1936.* New York: Long Island Historical Society, n.d.

Moore, William Luther. *The Literature of the American Negro Prior to 1865: An Anthology and a History, Vol II.* Washington: U.S. Office of Education, 1943.

National Anti-Slavery Standard. 1847-1848.

New York *Age.* 1890.

New York *Sun.* 1845-1846.

North Star. 1847-1850.

Plaindealer (Detroit). 1890.

The Ram's Horn. 1847.

Rights of All. 1829.

Rochester *Daily Advertiser.* 1847.

Russwurm, John B., to Col. John S. Russwurm, 9 January 1826. Original in Ms Section, Tennessee State Library and Archives; copy in Bowdoin College Library.

_____. "The Conditions and Prospects of Hayti." Commencement Address, Bowdoin College, 6 September 1826.

Walker, David. *Walker's Appeal, in Four Articles: Together with a Preamble, to the Colored Citizens of the World.* Boston: By the author, 1830.

Weekly Advocate. 1837.

Secondary Sources

Aptheker, Herbert, ed. *A Documentary History of the Negro People in the United States.* New York: The Citadel, 1951.

Barrow, Lionel C. Jr. "Our Own Cause: 'Freedom's Journal' and the Beginnings of the Black Press." *Journalism History* 4 (Winter 1977-78): 118-122.

Bennett, Lerone Jr. *Pioneers in Protest.* Chicago: Johnson Publishing Co. Inc., 1968.

Bryan, Carter R. "Negro Journalism in America Before Emancipation." *Journalism Monographs* 12 (September 1969): 1-33.

Dann, Martin E., ed. *The Black Press, 1827-1890: The Quest for National Unity.* New York: G.P. Putnam's Sons, 1971.

Detwiler, Frederick. *The Negro Press in the United States.* Chicago: University of Chicago Press, 1922.

Dorsey, H. Lewis. "Progress of Afro-American Journalism." Parsons (Kan.) *Weekly Blade*, 28 April 1894.

Finkle, Lee. *Forum for Protest.* Cranbury, N.J.: Associated University Presses, 1975.

Foner, Philip S., ed. *The Life and Writings of Frederick Douglass.* New York: International Publishers, 1950.

Gatewood, Willard B. Jr., ed. *Free Man of Color: The Autobiography of Willis Augustus Hodges.* Knoxville: University of Tennessee Press, 1982.

Gross, Bella. "'Freedom's Journal' and the 'Rights of All.'" *Journal of Negro History* 17 (July 1932): 241-286.

Hudson, Frederic. *Journalism in the United States, from 1690 to 1872.* New York: Harper and Row, 1873.

Jacobs, Donald M. "William Lloyd Garrison's *Liberator* and Boston's Blacks, 1830-1865." *New England Quarterly* 44 (June 1971): 259-277.

Kessler, Lauren. *The Dissident Press: Alternative Journalism in American History.* Beverly Hills: Sage Publications, 1984.

La Brie, Henry, III. "Black Newspapers: The Roots are 150 Years Deep." *Journalism History* 4 (Winter 1977-78): 111-113.

Mabee, Carleton. *Black Freedom: The Non-Violent Aboli-tionists from 1830 through the Civil War.* London: Macmillan & Co., 1970.

Mott, Frank Luther. *American Journalism.* New York: Macmillan, 1950.

Myrdal, Gunnar. *An American Dilemma: The Negro Prob-lem and Modern Democracy.* New York: Harper and Brothers Publishers, 1944.

Nordin, Kenneth. "In Search of Black Unity: An Interpreta-tion of the Content and Function of 'Freedom's Journal.'" *Journalism History* 4 (Winter 1977-78): 123-128.

Olbrich, Emil. *The Development of Sentiment on Negro Suf-frage to 1860.* Bulletin of the University of Wisconsin, 477, History Series, Vol. 3, no. 1. Madison: University of Wis-consin, 1921.

Pease, Jane H., and William H. Pease. *They Who Would Be Free: Blacks' Search for Freedom, 1830-1861.* New York: Atheneum, 1974.

Penn, Irving Garland. *The Afro-American Press and its Editors.* Springfield, Mass.: Wiley and Co., 1891.

Porter, Charles W. "The Black Press in America Before the Emancipation." M.A. thesis, University of Alabama, Tuscaloosa, 1970.

Pride, Armistead. "'Rights of All': Second Step in the Devel-opment of Black Journalism." *Journalism History* 4 (Winter 1977-78): 129-131.

Quarles, Benjamin. *Frederick Douglass*. Washington, D.C.: The Associated Publishers, Inc., 1948.

Rollins, F.A. *Life and Public Service of Martin R. Delaney*. Hartford, Conn.: Park Publishing Co., 1883.

Sanborn, F.B., ed. *The Life and Letters of John Brown*. Boston: Roberts Brothers, 1891.

Suggs, Henry Lewis, ed. *The Black Press in the South, 1865-1979*. Westport, Conn.: Greenwood Press, 1983.

Tappan, Lewis. *Life of Arthur Tappan*. New York: Hurd and Houghton, 1870.

Tinney, James S., and Justine J. Rector, eds. *Issues and Trends in Afro-American Journalism*. Lanham, Md.: University Press of America, 1980.

Wolseley, Roland. *The Black Press, U.S.A.* Ames: Iowa State University Press, 1971.

Woodson, Carter G. *The Education of the Negro Prior to 1861*. New York, 1915.

_____. *Negro Orators and Their Orations*. New York: Russell and Russell, 1969.

INDEX